FIT FOR A KING™

THE ELVIS PRESLEY COOKBOOK

FIT FOR A KING™

THE ELVIS PRESLEY COOKBOOK

Elizabeth McKeon, Ralph Gevirtz & Julie Bandy

RUTLEDGE HILL PRESS
NASHVILLE, TENNESSEE

From *Elvis World* by Jane and Michael Stern. Copyright © 1987 by Jane and Michael Stern. Reprinted by permission by Alfred A. Knopf, Inc.
From *"E" Is for Elvis* by Caroline Lathan and Jeanne Sakol. Copyright © 1990 by Caroline Latham and Jeanne Sakol, text and illustrations. Used by permission of New American Library, a division of Penguin Books USA, Inc.
All Shook Up Elvis Day-By-Day 1954-1977 by Lee Cotton. Copyright © 1985. Published by Pierian Press. Reprinted by permission from Popular Cultural, Inc.
Mystery Train: Images of American Rock 'n' Roll Music by Greil Marcus. Copyright © 1975 E. P. Dutton and Company, Inc. Page 226.

Published in Nashville, Tennessee, by Rutledge Hill Press, 513 Third Avenue South, Nashville, Tennessee 37210. Distributed in Canada by H. B. Fenn & Company, Ltd., Mississauga, Ontario.

Typography by D&T/Bailey, Nashville, Tennessee
Design by Harriette Bateman

Library of Congress Cataloging-in-Publication Data

McKeon, Elizabeth, 1962–
    Fit for a king : the Elvis Presley cookbook / Elizabeth McKeon,
Ralph Gevirtz & Julie Bandy.
      p. cm.
    Includes index.
    ISBN 1-55853-196-3
    1. Cookery, American—Southern style. 2. Presley, Elvis,
1935–1977. I. Gevirtz, Ralph, 1958– . II. Bandy, Julie, 1956–
III. Title.
TX715.2.S68M34 1992   92-25266
641.5975—dc20   CIP

Printed in the United States of America
  3 4 5 6 7 8 9 — 97 96 95 94 93 92

Printed by Vaughan Printing

☆ **ELVIS taking time out to read a fan magazine**

ACKNOWLEDGMENTS

When one thinks about Elvis Presley, one doesn't necessarily think about cooking or, for that matter, a cookbook. We didn't either at first. The concept for this cookbook came about when we thought about Elvis Presley and where he chose to live.

But undertaking this book involved more than we anticipated, and we would like to thank the many people who helped us through the project: Harriet Stockanes, our permissions editor, who got the ball rolling for us; C. Barry Ward, attorney for the Presley Estate, who gave us the final go-ahead; Jaques Dulin, whose patience and confidence in us was never less than 100 percent; Irene Maleti, president of the "King of Our Hearts Elvis Presley Fan Club," and her husband, Sam, for pointing us in the right direction; a very special thank you to Linda Everett, who opened her photo albums of Elvis and shared the many treasures hidden inside; Alvena Roy for sharing her recipes and memories of Elvis; and Carol and Trudy for getting us past the finish line.

We would also like to thank our many friends who encouraged us every step of the way, especially Anne, who gave us the idea for the title; and Jon, for his patience during those many late night phone calls about the manuscript and his help with the index; Bernie, Lewis, Charlie, and Debbie, who were there from the beginning; Richard, Margaret, Dorre, and Meiko, who stood by with support during the many months of editing and rewriting.

And the greatest thank you to our families, especially Ronnie and Bonnie for their special loving, listening, and support; Treva and Joretta for their unconditional support; Stephen, Kathy, and Mike for being the best a sister could ever have; a big thank you to Madeleine and Molly, who have been extremely good to us the past two years; and to our parents, who taught us to take a chance and gave us the support and love to do so.

A special thank you to Ron Pitkin, his wife, Julie, and Larry Stone at Rutledge Hill Press for their patience and helpful guidance in getting this book off the ground and believing in our idea from the start.

And lastly to Elvis, for giving us over thirty years of magic. And to his many fans who continue to keep that magic alive.

—Thanks to you all!

ONTENTS

☆ **ADMIRING a guitar-shaped birthday cake at Graceland**

ELVIS PRESLEY

*I*n keeping with the traditions of the American Dream, it is no surprise that Elvis Aron Presley was born into poverty on January 8, 1935, in East Tupelo, Mississippi.

Remembering those hard times, Elvis made a promise to his mother that when he grew up they would never be poor again. What followed was a series of events that undoubtedly helped him to keep that promise.

The first was his exposure to music at a young age while attending church. The second was a $12.95 guitar he received as a gift. And the third was when he moved with his mother and father to Memphis, Tennessee.

While attending L.C. Humes high school, Elvis made plenty of friends. His polite, shy country ways also earned him the respect of his teachers. It was this charm that would continue into his days as one of the world's most influential entertainers.

Elvis helped to support his family by working a variety of odd jobs, including as a truck driver and movie usher. With his busy schedule, he still found the time to sing in the school's annual Christmas concert.

In July of 1953, he walked into the Memphis Recording Studio and recorded "My Happiness" and "That's When Your Heartache Begins." It was to be a birthday gift for his mother, Gladys. The owner of the studio, Sam Phillips, had Elvis come back to record "Casual Love Affair" and "I'll Never Stand in Your Way." It was now apparent that the many hours Elvis had spent in front of the radio, mimicking the songs he heard, was about to pay off. As one critic would later say, "Elvis has set the music world afire."

In the summer of 1954 Elvis linked up with Scotty Moore and Bill Black, forming a group called The Blue Moon Boys. They performed at county fairs and local clubs. For the first time, Elvis was making money from his unique style of music.

Eventually Elvis met up with Colonel Tom Parker, who became his lifelong manager. It was the Colonel who exposed Elvis's unique talents to the world. In November 1955, the Colonel negotiated a deal with RCA to buy Elvis's contract from Sun Records. In January of 1956, "Heartbreak Hotel" hit the airwaves followed by "Blue Suede Shoes."

The more public Elvis became, the more his fans screamed for him. There were also the loud outcries warning of Elvis's "bad influence" on the nation's youth by civic leaders and various church groups. But Elvis's fans increased with such rapidly growing numbers that in 1956 *Variety* magazine crowned him the "King of Rock and Roll."

The next step for Elvis was television. From the first time he appeared in living rooms across the nation, his popularity soared.

Elvis Presley

From there, Hollywood beckoned, and Elvis jumped to the big screen. Elvis's first film, *Love Me Tender*, released by 20th Century Fox, earned him a million dollars. The critics panned Elvis's acting ability, but his fans loved him. Fan clubs sprouted up all over the globe, and Elvis received as many as five thousand letters a day.

In late 1957, with his career in full swing, Elvis received his draft notice from the U.S. Army. To make sure he would not be forgotten while stationed in Germany, the Colonel had Elvis record music that was to be released during his absence. While he was training in Texas, the word came that his mother had passed away. Her death was a blow to Elvis. Also while stationed in Germany Elvis met Priscilla Beaulieu.

Upon Elvis's return to the United States, the Colonel lined up a guest appearance for him on Frank Sinatra's television special. It was the Colonel's way of letting the fans know that Elvis was back in action. This was followed by the film release of *G.I. Blues.*

Gossip columnists were now linking Elvis romantically with his leading ladies, but it was Priscilla who captured Elvis's heart. In 1960 she spent Christmas with him at Graceland. During their long courtship, Elvis continued to record songs that turned into gold records as well as make movies in Hollywood. With more than enough money rolling in, Elvis donated a considerable amount to various charities. For himself he bought expensive cars and jewelry.

On May 1, 1967, Elvis and Priscilla were married in a private ceremony held in Las Vegas. Nine months later, Elvis became a father. Of his daughter, Lisa Marie, Elvis said, "One of the greatest moments of my life comes when she looks up and smiles just for me."

As Priscilla and Lisa Marie settled into life at Graceland, Elvis continued to perform in concert, record music, and make movies. Priscilla, who grew tired of the somewhat lonely lifestyle, separated from Elvis in 1972. A year later their divorce was final.

With the failure of his marriage, Elvis poured himself into his work. Plagued by ill health, he would not slow down for fear of disappointing his fans. In August of 1977 Elvis returned to Graceland to rest before his next series of concert appearances. On August 16, he died at the age of forty-two. The news of his death shocked the world. Millions mourned the country boy who became the King. Although his death has created an absence in the entertainment industry, millions continue to enjoy his music and films. And for his fans, Elvis left a legacy to be cherished.

INTRODUCTION

*M*ention Elvis, and most everyone knows who you are talking about. Mention "The King," and the response is generally the same. It is evident, from all that has ever been said or written about Elvis Presley, that he was, and is, a legend.

It began in July of 1953, when he recorded "My Happiness" and "That's When Your Heartache Begins" at the Memphis Recording Studio, later known as Sun Records. That summer was just the beginning of a career that would span across three decades.

Aside from all the fame, fortune, and recognition that Elvis achieved during his lifetime, he never once forgot where he came from and the values instilled in him by his southern upbringing.

Born in East Tupelo, Mississippi, he moved with his family to Memphis, Tennessee, when he was thirteen years old. From that moment on, he made Memphis his home.

At the age of twenty-one, he bought Graceland, a traditional southern mansion. In the evenings Elvis would stroll down to the front gates to talk with his fans. His charming, warm hospitality was neither compromised nor abandoned by his sudden, sustained wealth and popularity. He shared with others, especially with family and friends who were most important to him.

For Elvis it was not uncommon to have them over for dinner. They would gather around the formal dining room to share in a simple meal together. Often prepared were a variety of dishes, many like the ones he enjoyed as a young boy.

Here now is a collection of recipes popular during the time Elvis was living at Graceland. Some are from Alvena Roy, his longtime cook. Others are for foods he ate regularly, and yet others are for foods he likely served the many guests at his generous table. With them, we hope that you too will create traditional, wholesome, home-cooked meals for your family and friends, and that you will enjoy the same warmth in your home as Elvis did at Graceland.

—*Elizabeth McKeon, Ralph Gevirtz, and Julie Bandy*

ELVIS'S PANTRY

THE FOLLOWING is a list of items that were kept on hand in the kitchen, for Elvis, at all times.

- *Fresh, lean, unfrozen ground meat*
- *One case regular Pepsi*
- *One case orange drinks*
- *Rolls (hot rolls—Brown 'n' Serve)*
- *Cans of biscuits (at least six)*
- *Hamburger buns*
- *Pickles*
- *Potatoes and onions*
- *Assorted fresh fruit*
- *Cans of sauerkraut*
- *Wieners*
- *At least three bottles of milk, including half & half*
- *Thin, lean bacon*
- *Mustard*
- *Peanut butter*
- *Fresh, hand-squeezed cold orange juice*
- *Banana pudding (to be made each night)*
- *Ingredients for meat loaf and sauce*
- *Brownies*
- *Ice Cream—vanilla and chocolate*
- *Shredded coconut*
- *Fudge cookies*
- *Gum (Spearmint, Doublemint, Juicy Fruit—three of each)*

$\mathscr{F}$OREWORD

$\mathscr{I}$n the spring of 1963 my cousin was working for Elvis Presley at his Bel Air home on Perugia Way. She had heard there was an opening for a cook's position and told me of the opportunity. I met with Elvis Presley, and on May 17, 1963, I went to work for him.

Initially I was quite nervous, but I was soon put at ease by Elvis's warm charm and great sense of humor.

Many exciting events took place during the time I cooked for Elvis. One was when the Beatles visited during their U.S. tour in August 1965. I prepared a midnight supper that included broiled chicken livers wrapped in bacon, sweet and sour meatballs, deviled eggs, fresh cracked crab, fruit, and a platter of assorted cold cuts and cheeses.

In September 1965 Elvis moved to Rocca Way, near the Bel Air Hotel. Like the other places Elvis lived, his fans camped out near the front gates just to catch a glimpse of him. When the weather was warm, he would send out glasses of cold lemonade and iced tea.

In the spring of 1967 when it was announced that Elvis and Priscilla would marry, I went to the Palm Springs house to prepare for the May 1 wedding. The menu for the guests was turkey with stuffing and gravy, string beans, and stuffed tomatoes. And of course there was the six-tiered wedding cake decorated with white pearls and red hearts. For "his boys" Elvis had me cook up a batch of spaghetti with French bread.

In October of that year Elvis asked me to accompany him to Sedona, Arizona, where he was making *Stay Away Joe*. During the time we were on location, I prepared many of Elvis's favorite dishes because he preferred home-cooked meals to those available in the studio commissary.

In December Elvis asked me to cook Christmas dinner for him at Graceland. He insisted on a traditional Christmas dinner for his guests. For himself, he asked me to prepare ham salad, potato salad, meat loaf, hot rolls, and plenty of monkey bread.

One of the biggest highlights occured on February 1, 1968, when Lisa Marie, was born. It was a joy and an honor to look after Lisa until she was three months old.

As I look back to when I worked for Elvis Presley as his cook, I become somewhat sentimental. It was a pleasure, and I will cherish those memories forever. I hope that these recipes will create new memories. I am now retired and living in Southern California in the home Elvis bought for me.

—Alvena Roy
January 1992
Los Angeles, California

*T WAS widely known that Elvis loved
Western films. He often rented a Memphis theater after hours so
he and his friends could watch Westerns all night. At dawn they
would stop at a nearby restaurant for breakfast or would go to
Graceland where Gladys, his mother, would prepare griddle cakes
and hominy grits for all of them.*

Fit For a King

ℳenus

The menus suggested here are just that, suggestions. You may want to vary them, exercising your own imagination. The combination for any menu is endless. These menus are only a guide to help you get started. All of these menus were created from those dishes that Elvis especially enjoyed.

"LET'S HAVE A PARTY"

Garlic Dip
Stuffed Celery
Deviled Eggs
Fried Cheese Balls
Sweet and Sour Meatballs
Tomato Juice Cocktail

EARLY RISER BREAKFAST

Coffee and Tea
Orange Juice
Hominy Grits
Pan-Fried Potatoes
Blueberry Muffins
Griddle Cakes
Spanish Omelette

MORNINGS IN MEMPHIS

Coffee and Tea
Orange Juice
Hash Brown Potatoes
Baking Powder Biscuits
Melon Salad
French Toast
Scrambled Eggs

---

*T*WO WEEKS *before Elvis was to leave for the army, his mother invited his friends over to Graceland for a farewell party. Making sure there was plenty for everybody to eat, she prepared Elvis's favorite pork chops with mashed potatoes and gravy. For dessert everyone enjoyed her homemade apple pie.*

SUNDAY BRUNCH

Coffee and Tea
Tomato Juice Cocktail
Green Pea Salad
Fruit Salad
Cranberry Roast Pork
Crispy Fried Chicken
Buttermilk Biscuits
Apple Pie

THE GLADYS SPECIAL

Vegetable Soup
Potato Salad
Bacon and Tomato Sandwich
Fudge Cookies
Lemonade

NEVER FAIL FAVORITE LUNCH

Milk
Peanut Butter and Banana Sandwich
Lemon Meringue Pie

HIGH NOON

Vegetable Soup
Cheeseburger
Pound Cake
Banana Pudding
Chocolate Malted Shake

LUNCH COUNTER SPECIAL

Chicken Salad
Pear Salad
Strawberry Ice Cream
Cherry Pie
Milk

COMPANY'S COMING

Coffee and Tea
Baking Powder Biscuits
Symphony of Green Salad
Fried Okra
Mashed Potatoes and Gravy
Pork Chops with Sauerkraut
Apple Pie

SUNDAY SUPPER

Coffee and Tea
Corn Bread
Vegetable Soup
Mustard Greens and Potatoes
Fried Okra
Meat Loaf
Coconut Cake

A SOUTHERN FEAST

Coffee and Tea
Cole Slaw
Potato Salad
Crispy Fried Chicken
Corn Bread
Peach Cobbler
Pecan Pie

A PICNIC IN THE PARK

Cole Slaw
Potato Salad
Deviled Eggs
Baked Beans
Cheeseburgers
Lemonade

☆ **ENJOYING a day of sunshine**

FAMILY BARBECUE

Cole Slaw
Hush Puppies
Ham Salad
Fried Okra
Maple Spareribs
Strawberry Ice Cream
Pineapple Soda

GARDEN PARTY

Stuffed Celery
Deviled Eggs
Corn Bread
Green Pea Salad
Cornish Game Hens
Peanut Butter Pie

LAS VEGAS SPECIAL

Vegetable Soup
Baking Powder Biscuits
Baked Beans
Crispy Fried Chicken
Chocolate Malted Shake
Blueberry Pie

A JANUARY BIRTHDAY BASH

Cheeseburgers
Porkchops with Sauerkraut
Mashed Potatoes and Gravy
Peanut Butter and Banana Sandwich
Coconut Cake
Chocolate Malted Shake

&LVIS was always home with his family at Graceland for Christmas. There would be plenty of packages under the huge tree. He served the traditional turkey with stuffing, but for himself, Elvis preferred ham salad, potato salad, meat loaf, and monkey bread.

CHRISTMAS IN MEMPHIS

Coffee and Tea
Baking Powder Biscuits
Vegetable Soup
Green Pea Salad
Cranberry Squash
Turkey with Stuffing and Gravy
Apple Pie

☆ **IN MEMPHIS with friend at age thirteen**

*E*LVIS PRESLEY *was born around noon on
January 8, 1935, in the farm community of East Tupelo, Mississippi. In
this town of 11,000 there was a movie theater, a department store,
cotton mills, a Carnation Milk plant, and textile plants.
His mother, Gladys, worked as a seamstress, and his father, Vernon,
was a carpenter. They lived as sharecroppers in a two-room shotgun
house, and they attended the First Assembly of God Church. For
entertainment they would sing on their front porch or hang out
down at the local grocery store.*

$\mathscr{A}$PPETIZERS

$\mathscr{M}$ango Chutney Pinwheels

½ cup Montrachet cheese   12 slices ham
⅓ cup mango chutney

■ In a blender combine the cheese and chutney, and process until the mixture is smooth. On waxed paper lay each slice of meat out flat. Spread a thin, even layer of the cheese mixture on each slice. Roll each slice tightly and arrange in a dish. Cover with aluminum foil and refrigerate for about 1 hour.

Cut each roll into 3 equal pieces before serving.

Makes 3 dozen.

$\mathscr{B}$read & Butter Pickles

10 medium cucumbers, sliced   1½ cups sugar
 6 medium onions, peeled and   2 teaspoons celery seed
   sliced   1 teaspoon mustard seed
 ½ cup salt   1 teaspoon ground ginger
 2 cups vinegar   ½ teaspoon turmeric
 2 cups water

■ In a large mixing bowl combine the cucumber and onion slices. Add the salt and let the mixture stand for about 2 hours.

In a saucepan combine the remaining ingredients and bring just to boiling over medium heat. Drain and rinse the cucumbers and onions, and add to the saucepan. Simmer for about 30 minutes or until tender. Pack in 3 sterilized pint jars.

Makes 3 pints.

$\mathscr{S}$ tuffed Celery

Cream Cheese Filling
1½ ounces cream cheese, softened
  2 tablespoons mayonnaise
  4 pimiento-stuffed olives, chopped
2 tablespoons pecans, finely
  chopped
Salt to taste

Blended Cheese Filling
  3 ounces cream cheese, softened
  1 tablespoon Roquefort cheese
1 tablespoon butter
Salt to taste

Egg Filling
  1 hard-boiled egg, finely chopped
  2 tablespoons mayonnaise
Salt and pepper to taste

  3 ribs crisp celery

■ In a small bowl combine the Cream Cheese Filling ingredients, blending thoroughly. Set aside.

In a separate bowl combine the Blended Cheese Filling ingredients, blending thoroughly. Set aside.

In a separate bowl combine the Egg Filling ingredients, blending well. Set aside.

Cut each rib of celery into 4 pieces. Mound Cream Cheese Filling onto 4 of the celery pieces. Mound Blended Cheese Filling onto 4 celery pieces. Mound the Egg Filling onto the remaining celery pieces. Refrigerate before serving.

Makes 12.

$\mathscr{N}$ ew Orleans Shrimp

  ⅓ cup oil
  2 tablespoons vinegar
  2 tablespoons mustard
  ½ teaspoon paprika
2 green onions, chopped
½ cup diced celery
2 cups cooked shrimp
Shredded lettuce

■ In a mixing bowl blend together all of the ingredients except the shrimp and lettuce. Gently fold in the cooked shrimp. Refrigerate for about 2 hours. Serve on beds of shredded lettuce.

Makes 4 servings.

Fit For a King

C heddar Cheese Sticks

3 loaves whole grain bread, very thinly sliced
4 jars Old English Cheese, softened
2 cups butter, softened

1 tablespoon Tabasco sauce
1 teaspoon onion powder
2 tablespoons chopped fresh dillweed
1½ teaspoons Worcestershire sauce

■ Remove the crusts from the bread and set it aside. In a mixing bowl blend the cheese with the butter, Tabasco, onion powder, dillweed, and Worcestershire sauce until the consistency of a smooth batter.

Divide the bread into stacks of 3 slices. Spread the mixture evenly between 3 slices and over the top. Repeat with the remaining stacks of bread. Cut each stack lengthwise into 4 equal sticks. Place on a baking sheet and freeze thoroughly.

Place the frozen sticks on a second baking sheet. Bake at 325° for about 30 minutes. Makes 7 dozen.

ELVIS'S earliest recollection of music was with his parents at the First Assembly of God Church. At the age of three he would run over to join the choir, singing the hymns. Although he didn't always know the words, he could carry a tune. After supper Gladys would teach him the words to the hymns, and the three of them would harmonize together.

G arlic Dip

1 clove garlic, minced
3 tablespoons garlic juice
4 ounces cream cheese, softened

1 cup sour cream
Raw vegetables or assorted crackers

■ In a mixing bowl blend the minced garlic with the garlic juice. Add the cream cheese and sour cream, blending thoroughly. Spoon the dip into a serving dish. Refrigerate before serving. Serve with raw vegetables or assorted crackers.

Makes about 2 cups.

ill Dip

2 cups sour cream	**1 tablespoon dried onion flakes**
2 cups mayonnaise	**1 teaspoon dillweed**
1 tablespoon chopped parsley	**Raw vegetables or assorted crackers**

■ In a mixing bowl blend the sour cream with the mayonnaise. In a separate bowl mix the parsley, dried onion flakes, and dillweed. Blend the dry ingredients into the sour cream mixture. Spoon the dip into a serving dish. Refrigerate overnight. Serve with raw vegetables or assorted crackers.

Makes 2 cups.

eviled Ham Dip

1 3-ounce can deviled ham	**1 teaspoon grated onion**
1 5-ounce jar pimiento cheese	**Assorted crackers or cubed bread**
½ cup mayonnaise	

■ Bring all of the ingredients to room temperature. In a mixing bowl blend the deviled ham with the mayonnaise. Add the pimiento cheese and onion. Spoon the dip into a serving dish. Serve with assorted crackers or cubed bread.

Makes 1½ cups.

hicken Livers Wrapped in Bacon

¾ pound chicken livers	**5 drops onion juice**
½ teaspoon salt	**6 slices bacon**
Pepper to taste	**1 tablespoon finely chopped parsley**

■ Clean the chicken livers thoroughly in cold water. Pat dry with paper towels. Lay the livers on wax paper. Sprinkle with salt, pepper, and onion juice.

Cut the bacon slices in half. Wrap each piece around a chicken liver. Fasten with a 4-inch skewer and place in a shallow pan lined with aluminum foil.

Broil for about 7 minutes or until the bacon is thoroughly cooked. Turn and brown the other side. Place on a platter and drain. Pour remaining pan juices over the livers. Sprinkle with parsley.

Makes 4 servings.

Fit For a King

 hrimp Cocktail

½ **pound fresh shrimp**
¾ **cup chili sauce**
 3 **tablespoons fresh lemon juice**
 3 **tablespoons prepared**
   horseradish
 2 **teaspoons Worcestershire sauce**

1 **teaspoon grated onion**
Tabasco sauce to taste
Salt and pepper to taste
Parsley
Lemon slices

■ Bring a saucepan of salted water to a boil. Cook the shrimp for about 15 minutes. Drain and clean, removing the shells and veins. Break into small pieces.

In a mixing bowl blend together the chili sauce, lemon juice, horseradish and Worcestershire sauce. Add the onion, Tabasco, salt, and pepper. Add shrimp and toss to coat. Serve in chilled cocktail glasses. Garnish with parsley and lemon slices.

Makes 4 servings.

☆ **ELVIS with his friends in Memphis**

Appetizers

lives Wrapped in Bacon

12 pimiento-stuffed olives　　　**6 slices bacon**

■ Cut bacon slices in half. Wrap each piece around an olive. Fasten with skewers and place in a shallow pan lined with aluminum foil.

Broil for about 4 minutes or until the bacon is thoroughly cooked. Turn and brown the other side. Place on a platter and let drain.

Makes 1 dozen.

ushrooms Stuffed with Crab

24 large mushrooms
　2 tablespoons chopped onion
　2 tablespoons butter
　1 teaspoon fresh lemon juice

1 egg, beaten
1 12-ounce can crab meat
¼ cup grated Monterey Jack cheese

Cream Sauce
　3 tablespoons butter
　4 tablespoons all-purpose flour
　1 cup cream
1½ cups half & half
　2 tablespoons grated Parmesan
　　cheese

½ cup grated Monterey Jack cheese
Salt and pepper to taste
1 clove garlic, minced

■ Remove the stems from the mushrooms and reserve the caps. Chop the stems and mix them with the chopped onion. In a skillet melt 2 tablespoons of butter and sauté the mushroom mixture until the onions are transparent. Remove the skillet from the heat. Add the lemon juice, egg, crab meat, and ¼ cup of Monterey Jack cheese. Fill the mushroom caps with the stuffing. Place the stuffed mushrooms in a 9 x 13-inch baking dish.

In the top of a double boiler over simmering water melt 3 tablespoons of butter. Gradually blend in the flour. Slowly add the remaining ingredients. Stir until the cheeses have melted. Pour the sauce over the mushrooms. Bake uncovered at 400° for about 20 minutes.

Makes 2 dozen.

Fit For a King

arbecue Sauce I

1 cup dry red wine	2 cloves garlic, minced
1 6-ounce can tomato paste	¼ teaspoon salt
¼ cup olive oil	½ teaspoon pepper
1½ teaspoons crushed oregano	

■ In a mixing bowl blend all of the ingredients in the order listed. Refrigerate any unused portion.

Makes about 2 cups.

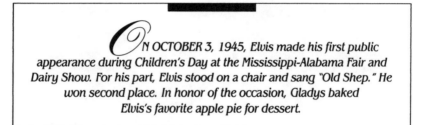

On OCTOBER 3, 1945, Elvis made his first public appearance during Children's Day at the Mississippi-Alabama Fair and Dairy Show. For his part, Elvis stood on a chair and sang "Old Shep." He won second place. In honor of the occasion, Gladys baked Elvis's favorite apple pie for dessert.

arbecue Sauce II

3½ cups ketchup	½ cup thick steak sauce
1½ cups chili sauce	Tabasco sauce to taste
⅓ cup mustard	¼ cup Worcestershire sauce
1 teaspoon dry mustard	1 tablespoon soy sauce
1½ cups light brown sugar, packed	1 tablespoon oil
1½ cups red wine vinegar	1½ cups beer
1 cup fresh lemon juice	

■ In a mixing bowl blend all of the ingredients in the order listed. Refrigerate any unused portion.

Makes about 12 cups.

Appetizers

Vegetable Dip

1 cup sour cream
½ cup mayonnaise
¼ cup chopped radishes
¼ cup chopped green bell pepper
¼ cup chopped green onion
¼ cup peeled and chopped carrots
¼ cup peeled and chopped cucumbers
1 tablespoon sugar
Salt and pepper to taste
Garlic powder to taste
Assorted crackers or cubed bread

■ In a mixing bowl blend together the sour cream and mayonnaise. Add the chopped vegetables, sugar, and seasonings. Refrigerate for about 1 hour. Serve with assorted crackers or cubed bread.

Makes about 3½ cups.

☆ TRYING to look like his idol James Dean

$\mathscr{B}$ eef Jerky

6 tablespoons soy sauce
6 tablespoons Worcestershire
  sauce
4 cloves garlic, minced
4 tablespoons sherry

1 teaspoon black pepper
½ teaspoon red pepper
1 2-pound London Broil, cut into
  ⅛-inch strips across the grain

■ In a large bowl mix all the ingredients in the order listed. Marinate the meat for about 24 hours. Place the meat on a rack and dry thoroughly for another 24 hours. The meat should feel dry and look dark brown.

Set the oven at the lowest temperature. Place the meat inside, keeping the oven door slightly ajar. Bake until the meat is thoroughly dry.

Makes 8 servings.

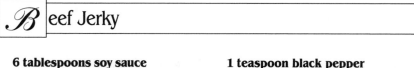

$\mathscr{E}$ LVIS loved to entertain his classmates.
They would sit on the grass in front of his house and listen to him
sing until it was time to go in for supper.

$\mathscr{S}$ hrimp Dip

1 10-ounce can condensed cream of
  shrimp soup
1 ¼-ounce envelope unflavored
  gelatin
3 tablespoons cold water
1 8-ounce package cream cheese,
  softened

1 cup mayonnaise
1 cup diced celery
1 pound shrimp
3 scallions, chopped
Raw vegetables or assorted crackers

■ In a saucepan melt the undiluted soup and cream cheese over low heat. In a cup soften the gelatin in the cold water. Stir to dissolve. Add the dissolved gelatin to the soup mixture. Blend in the mayonnaise, celery, shrimp, and scallions. Refrigerate for about 24 hours. Serve with raw vegetables or assorted crackers.

Makes about 6 cups.

Appetizers

$\mathscr{C}$ heese Fondue

4 cups bread cubes	**1 cup grated American cheese**
2½ cups milk	**Salt and pepper to taste**
4 eggs, separated	**Butter**

■ Butter a 2-quart casserole dish. Spread the cubed bread in the bottom of the prepared dish.

In a saucepan scald the milk. In a mixing bowl beat 3 egg yolks. Discard the remaining yolk. Add the cheese and seasonings. Fold the mixture into the scalded milk, stirring until the cheese has melted. Beat the egg whites until stiff and fold them into the cheese mixture. Pour the sauce over the bread cubes and dot with butter. Bake at 350° for about 30 minutes, or until the fondue is firm and golden brown. Serve warm.

Makes 4 to 6 servings.

$\mathscr{E}$LVIS *would sit for hours in front of the radio, listening to the "Grand Ole Opry." He learned the songs by imitating the notes on his guitar. When he knew the song, he would then add his own style to make it uniquely his own.*

---

our Cream Mustard Sauce

½ cup sour cream	**1 tablespoon fresh lemon juice**
1 teaspoon Worcestershire sauce	**1 tablespoon prepared horseradish**
¼ cup plain yogurt	**2 tablespoons minced parsley**
1 clove garlic, minced	**Raw or steamed vegetables**
4 tablespoons Dijon mustard	

■ In a mixing bowl blend all of the ingredients in the order listed, except the vegetables. Spoon the sauce into a serving dish. Serve with raw or steamed vegetables.

Fit For a King

$\mathcal{P}$ ecan-Cheese Ball

1 8-ounce package cream cheese, softened	1 clove garlic, minced
2 tablespoons steak sauce	Tabasco sauce to taste
1 cup chopped pecans	Raw vegetables or assorted crackers

■ In a mixing bowl blend all the ingredients in the order listed except the vegetables or crackers. Shape the cheese into a ball and place into a covered dish. Refrigerate for about 5 hours or until the mixture can hold its shape. Remove the cheese ball from refrigerator at least 25 minutes before serving. Serve with raw vegetables or assorted crackers.

Makes about 8 servings.

$\mathcal{S}$ weet & Sour Meatballs

Meatballs

⅓ cup bread crumbs	¾ pound ground beef
½ cup water	¼ pound ground pork
½ cup light cream	¾ teaspoon salt
3 tablespoons butter, softened	¾ teaspoon sugar
2 tablespoons finely chopped onion	¼ teaspoon pepper

Sweet and Sour Sauce

2 tablespoons cornstarch	¼ cup vinegar
½ teaspoon salt	1 cup pineapple juice
¼ cup packed light brown sugar	1 tablespoon soy sauce

■ In a large mixing bowl combine the bread crumbs, water, and cream. Set the mixture aside.

In a heavy skillet melt 1 tablespoon of butter and sauté the onion until transparent. Transfer the onion to a separate mixing bowl and add the ground beef and ground pork. Add the salt, sugar, pepper, and bread crumb mixture, blending well. Shape the meat into balls about ¾ inch in diameter.

In the same skillet melt 2 tablespoons of butter over medium heat. Brown the meatballs, turning frequently to brown evenly. Reduce the heat and cover. Continue to cook for about 10 minutes, turning frequently.

In a saucepan blend together the remaining ingredients. Cook over medium heat until thick, stirring constantly. Pour the sauce over the cooked meatballs.

Makes 4 dozen.

Appetizers

lmond Cheese Dip

1 cup grated American cheese   **⅓ cup toasted, chopped almonds**
4 teaspoons chopped green onions   **3 slices bacon, cooked and crumbled**
½ cup mayonnaise   **Raw vegetables or assorted crackers**
Salt to taste

■ In a mixing bowl blend the cheese with the onion and mayonnaise. Season with salt. Add the toasted almonds and crumbled bacon. Spoon the dip into a serving dish. Refrigerate about 2 hours. Serve with raw vegetables or assorted crackers.

☆ **ELVIS with his mother and father, Gladys and Vernon Presley**

C rab-Bacon Rolls

¼ cup tomato juice
1 egg, beaten
1 7-ounce can crab meat, drained
½ cup bread crumbs
½ tablespoon chopped parsley

1 tablespoon fresh lemon juice
Salt and pepper to taste
¼ teaspoon Worcestershire sauce
10 slices bacon, cut in half

■ In a mixing bowl blend together the tomato juice and egg. Add the crab meat, bread crumbs, parsley, lemon juice, and Worcestershire sauce. Season with salt and pepper.

Roll the dough out lengthwise, and cut into 20 equal portions. Wrap each with a piece of bacon and secure with toothpicks.

Broil for about 10 minutes, turning to brown the bacon evenly.

Makes 20 servings.

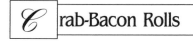

*A*S ELVIS got older, the Presleys began singing as a trio. They began in church, and since entertainment was hard to come by, their neighbors enjoyed listening to them. Soon they were invited to perform at meetings and camp revivals in and around Memphis.

D eviled Eggs

6 hard-boiled eggs
½ teaspoon salt
⅛ teaspoon pepper
¼ teaspoon dry mustard

1½ teaspoons apple cider vinegar
2 slices bacon
Paprika to taste

■ Fry the bacon until crisp. Drain and crumble. Peel the eggs when cool, and cut in half lengthwise. Remove the yolks, taking care not to tear the egg whites.

In a mixing bowl mash the yolks with the bacon and remaining ingredients. Blend until smooth. Pile the filling into the centers of the cooled egg whites. Sprinkle with paprika.

Makes 2 dozen.

Appetizers

lam-Cheese Dip

1 medium clove garlic, quartered
1 8-ounce can minced clams
6 ounces cream cheese, softened
1 teaspoon Worcestershire sauce

1 teaspoon fresh lemon juice
¼ teaspoon salt
Raw vegetables or assorted crackers

■ Rub the inside of a mixing bowl with the garlic. Drain and reserve the juice from the clams. Finely chop the clams. Add 1 tablespoon of the clam juice and the remaining ingredients except the vegetables or crackers, blending well. Spoon the dip into a serving dish. Cover and refrigerate about 2 hours. Serve with raw vegetables or assorted crackers.

Makes 2 cups.

 elery-Cheese Balls

1 cup finely chopped celery
3 ounces cream cheese, softened
Salt and papper to taste

1 tablespoon chopped parsley
Paprika

■ In a mixing bowl blend the celery with the cream cheese. Season with salt and pepper. Shape into 12 balls and roll in the parsley. Sprinkle with paprika. Arrange on a serving plate and refrigerate until firm.

Makes 1 dozen.

 acon-Spinach Hors d'Oeuvres

2 10-ounce packages frozen
  spinach
1 0.4-ounce package ranch-style
  salad dressing mix

6 green onions, chopped
6 slices crisp bacon, chopped
1 cup mayonnaise
3 large flour tortillas

■ Thaw and drain the spinach. In a mixing bowl combine the spinach, mayonnaise, ranch dressing, onions, and bacon. Spread the mixture evenly over the flour tortillas. Roll up and cut into 1-inch sections. Secure with a toothpick. Refrigerate the hors d'oeuvres overnight.

Makes 12.

Fit For a King

☆ **STANDING behind Sun Studios in Memphis**

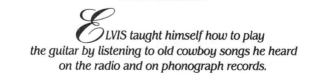

*Elvis taught himself how to play
the guitar by listening to old cowboy songs he heard
on the radio and on phonograph records.*

acon-Almond Dip

1 pound crisp bacon, chopped
Black pepper to taste
1 8-ounce package cream cheese,
  softened
Tabasco sauce to taste

1 cup sour cream
¼ cup chopped scallions
1 tablespoon chili sauce
½ cup slivered almonds
Raw vegetables or assorted crackers

■ In a mixing bowl blend all of the ingredients except the vegetables or crackers until somewhat chunky. Spoon into a serving dish. Refrigerate for about 1 hour. Serve with raw vegetables or assorted crackers.

    Makes about 5 cups.

HEN Elvis wanted a guitar for Christmas, he knew his parents could not afford it. His mother worked hard just to keep food on the table. It was then that Elvis promised his mother that when he got older, they would never be poor again and he would give her the things she deserved.

---

tuffed Mushrooms

24 large mushrooms, cleaned and
  dried
½ cup grated Swiss cheese
8 slices crisp bacon

1 medium onion, chopped
1 7¼-ounce can sliced black olives,
  chopped
¼ cup grated Parmesan cheese

■ Remove the stems from the mushrooms and reserve the caps. In a mixing bowl combine the Swiss cheese, bacon, onion, olives, and Parmesan cheese. Blend thoroughly.

    Stuff the mushroom caps with the cheese mixture, making sure that the filling is slightly mounded. Place the stuffed mushrooms on a baking sheet. Bake at 350° about 15 minutes, then broil for about 5 minutes more or until the filling is brown. Serve warm.

    Makes 2 dozen.

ried Cheese Balls

3 egg whites
1 tablespoon all-purpose flour
Salt to taste

1¾ cups grated Cheddar cheese
½ cup bread crumbs

■ In a mixing bowl beat the egg whites until stiff. In a separate mixing bowl blend the flour and salt. Add the flour with the cheese to the egg whites. Blend well. Drop by teaspoonfuls into the bread crumbs, coating well. Shape into balls.

Drop the balls into deep hot oil (375°) and fry for about 2 to 3 minutes or until golden. Drain on paper towels. Serve warm or cold.

Makes 2 dozen.

ush Puppies

½ cup sifted all-purpose flour
1 cup cornmeal
1 medium onion, chopped
1½ teaspoons baking powder

1 egg
1 teaspoon salt
1 teaspoon sugar
Milk

■ In a mixing bowl combine all of the ingredients, moistening with just enough milk to create a stiff dough. Drop the batter from a spoon into deep hot oil (350°) and fry for about 3 minutes, or until golden. Drain on paper towels. Serve warm.

Makes 2 dozen.

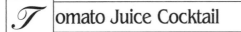omato Juice Cocktail

2½ cups tomato juice
1½ teaspoons finely chopped onion
1 teaspoon sugar

2 teaspoons fresh lemon juice
¼ teaspoon salt
¼ teaspoon Worcestershire sauce

■ In a blender mix all of the ingredients thoroughly. Strain and pour into a pitcher. Refrigerate until very chilled.

Makes 5 servings.

Appetizers

☆ **ELVIS back stage**

𝒫 epper-Stuffed Mushrooms

12 large mushrooms	**2 jalapeño peppers, chopped**
2 tablespoons olive oil	**⅔ cup grated Monterey Jack cheese**
2 small cloves garlic, minced	

■ Remove the stems from the mushrooms and reserve the caps. Finely chop the stems. In a skillet heat the oil over medium-low heat and sauté the mushroom caps for about 10 minutes. Drain on paper towels. In the oil remaining in the skillet sauté the chopped stems, garlic, and jalapeño peppers for about 10 minutes.

Transfer the mixture to a mixing bowl and add ½ cup of cheese, tossing until mixed. Fill the mushroom caps with the mixture, and top with the remaining cheese. Broil the stuffed mushrooms until the cheese melts and bubbles. Serve hot.

Makes 1 dozen.

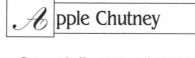pple Chutney

3 green bell peppers, chopped	3 cups apple cider vinegar
1 medium onion, chopped	1½ cups sugar
12 tart apples, peeled, cored, and	1½ teaspoons ginger
chopped	1½ cups grape jelly
1½ cups seedless raisins	¾ cup fresh lemon juice
1½ teaspoons salt	1 tablespoon grated lemon rind

■ In a large saucepan add the peppers, onion, apples, raisins, salt, vinegar, sugar, ginger, jelly, lemon juice, and lemon rind. Simmer over medium-low heat for about 1 hour or until thick. Pour into 4 pint jars and seal.

Makes 4 pints.

On SEPTEMBER 9, 1954, Elvis was paid ten dollars to perform at the grand opening of the Lamar-Airways Shopping Center. About 300 people attended the 9:00 P.M. performance. Elvis performed from a flat-bed truck parked in front of the new Katz Drug Store.

pinach Dip

½ cup chopped green onions	1 teaspoon dillweed
White pepper to taste	1 teaspoon oregano
½ cup chopped parsley	1 cup frozen spinach, thawed and
1 teaspoon fresh lemon juice	drained
1 cup sour cream	Raw vegetables or assorted crackers
1 cup mayonnaise	

■ In a mixing bowl combine the onions, pepper, and parsley. Add the lemon juice, sour cream, mayonnaise, dillweed, and oregano, blending well. Add the spinach, and mix thoroughly. Spoon the dip into a serving dish. Refrigerate for about 8 hours. Serve with raw vegetables or assorted crackers.

Makes about 4 cups.

☆ **THE FRONT entrance to Graceland**

*B*UILT *in 1939 and named for Grace Toof, the former owner's great aunt, Graceland had eighteen rooms, a four-car garage, and a yard full of mature trees and plantings. The land had been a Hereford cattle farm before the Presleys moved in. Whitehaven (not yet incorporated into Memphis) was still rolling country. The house ("one of Shelby County's most impressive," according to the Memphis Press-Scimitar story in 1957) had been on the market for quite some time. It was used as the annex by the local church and had been offered to the Memphis YMCA in early 1957 for $40,000. For Elvis Presley the price—for the house and the fourteen acres of surrounding land—was a cool $100,000.*

Fit For a King

Soups & Salads

Tomato Soup

3 tablespoons butter	2 leeks, chopped
2 tablespoons all-purpose flour	¼ cup lean cooked ham
2 cups beef stock	2 cups canned tomatoes
1 carrot, chopped	Salt and pepper to taste
2 ribs celery, chopped	1 tablespoon finely chopped chives
1 small turnip, chopped	

■ In a large saucepan melt 2 tablespoons of the butter. Blend in the flour. Add the beef stock, carrots, celery, turnips, leeks, and ham, and simmer for about 30 minutes. Add the tomatoes, and season with salt and pepper.

Slowly bring the soup to a boil, then simmer for about 20 minutes. Strain the soup through a sieve. Add the remaining butter and the chives.

Makes 4 cups.

Winter Soup

4 slices crisp bacon	½ cup diced celery
1 large onion, chopped	1 tablespoon white rice
2 14½-ounce cans chicken stock	1½ cups water
1 large potato, peeled and diced	Fresh parsley for garnish
1½ cups chopped green cabbage	

■ In a skillet fry the bacon. Add the chopped onion and sauté until transparent. Transfer to a saucepan, and add the chicken stock, potatoes, cabbage, celery, rice, and water.

Simmer until the potatoes are soft, about 30 minutes. Garnish with fresh parsley.

Makes 4 cups.

☆ GRACELAND in Memphis, Tennessee

B ean Soup

2 ounces salt pork, diced
¼ cup chopped onion
¼ cup all-purpose flour
1 quart water
2 cups diced potatoes
1 cup chopped celery
½ cup sliced carrots

2 cups canned tomatoes
1 teaspoon salt
1 cup canned navy beans
1 tablespoon chopped green bell
  pepper
½ tablespoon chopped parsley

■ In a saucepan fry the salt pork until brown. Add the onions and sauté. Blend in the flour. Slowly add the water and salt, stirring constantly. Add the remaining vegetables. Cover and cook until the vegetables are tender. Add the beans, and simmer for about 10 minutes. Add the pepper and parsley just before serving.

Makes 4 servings.

W HEN Elvis first saw Graceland
on a highway south of Memphis, it was being used by a church.
When he saw it was for sale, he promised that he would buy it
for his mother when he got the money.

$\mathscr{J}$ ambalaya

2 tablespoons oil	3 cups chicken broth
1 large onion, chopped	1 cup white rice
1 cup chopped green bell pepper	1 tablespoon chopped parsley
1 clove garlic, minced	½ teaspoon thyme
1 cup diced cooked chicken	½ teaspoon salt
1½ cups sliced smoked sausage	1 tablespoon hot pepper sauce
5 tomatoes, peeled and diced	1 cup cooked shrimp

■ In a large saucepan heat the oil. Sauté the onion, green pepper, and garlic until tender. Add the remaining ingredients except the shrimp, mix well, and bring to a boil. Cover and reduce the heat. Simmer for about 25 minutes or until the rice is cooked and the liquid has been absorbed. Add the shrimp and remove the pan from heat. Let the jambalaya stand for 5 minutes and mix again.

Makes 8 cups.

$\mathscr{S}$ plit Pea Soup

1 pound dried split peas	1 potato, peeled and sliced
1 pound pork	1 pound smoked sausage
2 bay leaves	Pepper to taste
1½ teaspoons salt	Tabasco sauce to taste
2 leeks, sliced	Dried celery leaves

■ Soak the peas overnight. In a saucepan cover the peas with three quarts of cold water. Bring to a boil. Add the pork, bay leaves, and salt. Cover the saucepan and simmer about 1 hour and 30 minutes, stirring occasionally. Add the leeks and potatoes, stirring frequently. Simmer for about 15 minutes, then add the sausage. Simmer for about 20 minutes more.

Remove the sausage and pork from the soup. Cut the skin from the pork and dice it into 1-inch cubes. Slice the sausage and return it with the pork to the soup. Season with pepper, Tabasco sauce, and dried celery leaves. Remove the bay leaves before serving.

Makes 8 cups.

Soups and Salads

 # otato Soup

3 cups peeled and diced potatoes	2 tablespoons all-purpose flour
4 carrots, peeled and sliced	2 cups milk
½ cup chopped onion	1 cup grated Parmesan cheese
1 small zucchini, peeled and cubed	6 slices bacon, cooked and crumbled
2 cups boiling water	Salt and pepper to taste
2 tablespoons butter	

■ In a saucepan combine the potatoes, carrots, onions, zucchini, and water. Simmer for about 15 minutes or until the vegetables are tender. Do not drain the water.

In a small saucepan melt the butter. Blend in the flour. Gradually add the milk, stirring constantly. Pour the white sauce into the vegetables. Blend in the cheese, and add the bacon. Heat until the cheese has completely melted. Season to taste.

Makes 4 cups.

☆ TALKING with fans outside the gates at Graceland

Fit For a King

$\mathscr{T}$ riple Mushroom Soup

5 dried black mushrooms	**3¼ cups half & half**
3 tablespoons butter	**3 sprigs parsley**
1 small onion, chopped	**½ teaspoon oil**
¼ pound fresh mushrooms	**Salt and pepper to taste**
3 tablespoons all-purpose flour	**Grated cheese for garnish**

■ Soak the dried mushrooms in water for about 30 minutes. Clean and remove the stems. In saucepan melt the butter over medium-low heat. Add the onions and sauté for about 2 minutes. Add the mushrooms. Cook until the liquid has evaporated. Blend in the flour and cook for 1 minute. Gradually stir in the half & half. Bring to a boil, stirring constantly.

Place the hot soup in a blender with the parsley, oil, salt, and pepper. Process until the mushrooms are chopped into fine bits. Return the soup to saucepan and reheat to boiling. Serve with grated cheese.

Serves 2.

$\mathscr{F}$ROM the moment Elvis moved into the mansion, he made it a point to spend time down at the front gates with his fans. There the crowd would gather around the King of Rock 'n' Roll, and Elvis—never in a hurry—would answer all of their questions.

$\mathscr{V}$ egetable Soup

1½ pounds shin of beef	**⅓ cup chopped cabbage**
2 quarts cold water	**⅓ cup diced celery**
½ cup chopped carrots	**⅓ cup shelled peas**
½ cup lima beans	**1½ teaspoons salt**
⅓ cup chopped onion	**Pepper to taste**

■ Wash the shin of beef and place it in a large saucepan. Cover with the cold water. Bring the water to a boil. Skim the fat off the top. Simmer for about 3 hours, or until the meat falls off the bone. Remove the meat from the broth and reserve it for another use.

Add the vegetables to the broth, and simmer until tender. Season with salt and pepper.

Makes 8 cups.

Soups and Salads

$\mathscr{C}$ ream of Onion Soup

2 slices bacon	**1⅔ cups evaporated milk**
1 cup sliced onion	**Salt and pepper to taste**
2 tablespoons all-purpose flour	**5 slices white bread toasted and**
3 cups water	**buttered**

■ In a soup pot fry the bacon. Do not overcook it. Add the onion and flour, stirring until the flour is blended with the bacon drippings. Gradually add the water. Stir until the mixture is smooth.

Cover and simmer for about 15 minutes or until the onions are tender. Add the milk, salt, and pepper. Reheat, uncovered, to boiling.

Place a slice of toasted, buttered bread in the bottom of each of 5 soup bowls. Pour in the hot soup.

Makes 5 servings.

$\mathscr{T}$HERE wasn't anything Elvis wouldn't buy for his mother. Sometimes she had to tell him not to buy her so many expensive things, but he always wanted her to have the best, especially for the house. After he had given her the gifts, they would go into the kitchen and eat Elvis's favorite bacon and tomato or fried peanut butter and banana sandwiches that she had prepared for him.

$\mathscr{H}$ am Salad

2½ cups cubed cooked ham	**1 tablespoon prepared mustard**
1 cup diced celery	**1 tablespoon chopped sweet pickles**
1 tablespoon fresh lemon juice	**⅛ teaspoon pepper**
½ cup mayonnaise	**Salt to taste**

■ In a large mixing bowl combine all of the ingredients. Toss thoroughly. Transfer the salad to a serving bowl. Refrigerate about 2 hours.

Makes 6 servings.

$\mathscr{S}$ ymphony of Green Salad

1 3-ounce package lime gelatin
1 cup hot water
2 cups small curd cottage cheese
1 9-ounce can crushed pineapple,
   drained

⅓ cup mayonnaise
2 tablespoons fresh lemon juice
⅓ cup peeled and diced cucumber
½ cup chopped walnuts

■ Dissolve the gelatin in the hot water. Pour the gelatin into a 6-cup mold. Refrigerate the gelatin until it thickens. Blend in the cottage cheese, pineapple, mayonnaise, and lemon juice. Add the cucumber and walnuts. Refrigerate the salad for about 7 hours, until firm.

Makes 12 servings.

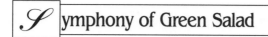

INNIE MAE, a tall, lanky woman lacking the softness that is stereotypical of grandmothers, liked to reminisce about her famous grandson's childhood in rural Mississippi.
"My Grandmother cooks all my favorite dishes," Elvis told reporters.
"You know, good, simple foods."

$\mathscr{S}$ even Layer Salad

1 head lettuce, shredded
¾ cup diced celery
⅓ cup sliced green bell pepper
¼ cup sliced red onion
1 10-ounce package frozen peas,
   thawed and drained

2 cups mayonnaise
3 teaspoons sugar
1 cup grated Romano cheese

■ In a large salad bowl layer the first 5 ingredients in the order listed. Do not toss. Spread with the mayonnaise and sprinkle with sugar. Top with grated Romano cheese. Cover tightly and refrigerate overnight. Before serving toss thoroughly.

Makes 8 servings.

Soups and Salads

 trawberry & Asparagus Salad

4 cups fresh strawberries	**1 bunch fresh asparagus**
Balsamic vinegar	**Olive oil**
Sugar to taste	**Salt and pepper to taste**

Vinaigrette dressing
1 tablespoon vinegar   **Salt and pepper to taste**
3 tablespoons olive oil

■ Wash and hull the strawberries. Drain and place them in a deep bowl. Sprinkle with vinegar and sugar and toss gently. Cover with plastic wrap and refrigerate. Occasionally stir the strawberries, making sure not to bruise them. Snap off the hard bottoms of asparagus spears and peel the ends. Steam to the desired crispness.

Place the dried asparagus spears in the center of a large platter and arrange the strawberries around the spears. Mix the dressing ingredients and pour over the berries and asparagus.

Makes 8 servings.

---

*WHILE he was stationed in Germany,
Elvis often spoke of being homesick. But even the thought
of Graceland always brought a smile to his face.*

---

aesar Salad

1 small clove garlic, minced	**1 tablespoon Worcestershire sauce**
3 anchovy fillets (plus oil)	**Salt and pepper to taste**
½ cup olive oil	**¾ cup grated Mozzarella cheese**
2 tablespoons white wine vinegar	**2 small heads Romaine lettuce, torn**
2 tablespoons fresh lemon juice	**1 cup croutons**
1 teaspoon mustard	**6 slices bacon, cooked and crumbled**
Tabasco sauce to taste	**½ cup grated Parmesan cheese**

■ In the bottom of a large wooden salad bowl combine the garlic and anchovy fillets. Mash with a wooden spoon. Blend in the olive oil, anchovy oil, vinegar, lemon juice, mustard, Tabasco, Worcestershire sauce, salt, pepper, and Mozzarella cheese.

Just before serving add the Romaine lettuce, and toss with dressing. Add the croutons, bacon, and Parmesan cheese.

Makes 8 servings.

𝒫 otato Salad

2 pounds small new potatoes, peeled	¾ cup mayonnaise
1 onion, chopped	1 tablespoon mustard
2 hard-boiled eggs, chopped	3 tablespoons sweet pickle juice
1 cup diced celery	Salt and pepper to taste

■ Boil the potatoes in salted water until tender. Drain and cool. Evenly slice the potatoes and place them in a large salad bowl. Add the onion, eggs, and celery.

In a separate bowl blend the mayonnaise, mustard, pickle juice, salt, and pepper. Toss the mayonnaise mixture into the potatoes. Refrigerate about 3 hours.

Makes 8 servings.

𝒪 range Spinach Salad

1 pound raw spinach	1 4-ounce can mandarin orange slices, drained
¼ pound mushrooms, sliced	2 hard-boiled eggs
1 3-ounce can of water chestnuts, sliced and drained	2 slices bacon, cooked and crumbled

Dressing

¼ cup oil	¼ teaspoon salt
2 tablespoons vinegar	1 teaspoon soy sauce
2 tablespoons fresh orange juice	Tabasco sauce to taste
¼ tablespoon dry mustard	

■ Clean and dry the spinach, and break the leaves into pieces. In a bowl toss together the spinach, mushrooms, water chestnuts, orange slices, eggs, and bacon. Combine the ingredients for the dressing. Toss the dressing into salad. Refrigerate for about 1 hour.

Makes 4 servings.

 aked Bananas

4 bananas	**Butter**
Fresh lemon juice	**Chopped walnuts**
Sugar	

■ Peel bananas and cut in half lengthwise. Place in a buttered baking dish. Sprinkle with fresh lemon juice. Bake at 350° for about 15 minutes.

Remove the bananas from the oven and sprinkle with sugar. Return them to the oven and bake for about 5 minutes more. Before serving, top with walnuts.

Makes 4 servings.

☆ HOLDING a wooden soldier, a gift from a female contestant who
won a "date" with Elvis in Bad Nauheim, Germany

Fit For a King

☆ TAKING a stroll around the grounds of his house in
Bad Nauheim, Germany

$\mathscr{C}$ ole Slaw

½ cup chopped onions
1 small head cabbage, chopped
2 teaspoons sugar
3 tablespoons water

½ teaspoon vinegar
Mayonnaise to taste
Salt to taste

■ In a mixing bowl toss the onion and cabbage. Add the sugar, water, and vinegar. Blend with the desired amount of mayonnaise. Add the salt, and mix well. Transfer the slaw to a serving bowl. Refrigerate about 3 hours.

Makes 6 cups.

Soups and Salads

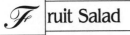ruit Salad

1 medium honeydew melon   **1 cup pineapple chunks**
1 cup pitted cherries   **2 tablespoons lime juice**
1 cup strawberries

■ Cut the honeydew melon in half lengthwise, and scoop out the seeds. Cut the cherries and strawberries in half. In a bowl toss the fruit with the pineapple chunks. Pour equal amounts into the center of the scooped out melon halves. Sprinkle lime juice over the fruit. Refrigerate until chilled before serving.

Makes 2 servings.

roccoli Salad

1 bunch broccoli   **1 cup raisins**
1 15-ounce can kidney beans,   **1 tablespoon sugar**
   drained   **1 tablespoon apple cider vinegar**
1 small red onion, chopped   **1 cup mayonnaise**

■ Cut the broccoli into bite-size chunks and set aside. In a salad bowl combine the kidney beans, onions, raisins, sugar, and vinegar. Toss well. Blend in the mayonnaise. Add the broccoli chunks, and mix thoroughly. Refrigerate before serving.

Makes 4 cups.

ingered Waldorf Salad

⅓ cup mayonnaise   **1 pear, diced**
1 tablespoon milk   **1 cup green seedless grape halves**
2 teaspoons fresh lemon juice   **½ cup diced celery**
¾ teaspoon ginger   **½ cup chopped pecans**
1 apple, peeled, cored, and diced

■ In a medium bowl blend the mayonnaise, milk, lemon juice, and ginger. Add the remaining ingredients, mixing thoroughly. Refrigerate for about 2 hours.

Makes 6 servings.

𝒲ilted Spinach Salad

2 bunches fresh spinach   **3 tablespoons sugar**
6 slices bacon   **2 tablespoons cider vinegar**

■ Wash the spinach and pat it dry. Remove the stems and tear the larger leaves into bite-size pieces. Cut the bacon into half inch strips, and sauté until crisp. Drain and reserve the excess fat.

In a large saucepan combine the sugar, vinegar, and 3 tablespoons of bacon fat. Bring the mixture to a boil, and cook until the sugar has dissolved.

Add the spinach and sauté, tossing rapidly, until the leaves are well coated with the dressing and begin to wilt. Transfer the salad to a serving bowl. Serve immediately.

Makes 4 cups.

☆ **ENJOYING a bowl of soup in Germany**

☆ **AT GRACELAND upon his return from Germany**

ELVIS said that when he first saw Graceland after coming home from Germany, his heart skipped a beat. He was home again—finally—in his old-style southern mansion.

ℰ gg Salad

6 hard-boiled eggs	**½ cup diced celery**
¼ cup chopped bread and butter	**Salt and pepper to taste**
pickles	**Mayonnaise**
1 teaspoon mustard	**Shredded lettuce**

■ Peel and finely chop the eggs. In a mixing bowl blend the chopped eggs with the pickles, mustard, celery, salt, and pepper. Add mayonnaise to the desired consistency. Serve on beds of shredded lettuce.

Makes 4 servings.

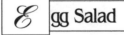

 ea & Cucumber Salad

1 medium cucumber   **Dillweed to taste**
2 pounds fresh green peas, shelled **Sour cream to taste**
Butter to taste   **Salt and pepper to taste**

■ Remove and discard the ends of the cucumber. Peel and remove the seeds. Cut into quarters. Cut each quarter in half lengthwise, then cut into ¼-inch chunks. Drop into boiling salted water.

Return the water to a boil. Add the peas, and cook until both are tender but not soft. Drain. Add the butter, dillweed, sour cream, salt, and pepper. Toss well.

Makes 4 servings.

*HEN asked if he would ever sell Graceland,
Elvis said he would never do it. He had bought it for his mother, and it
was hers to keep. "This is home," he said.*

$\mathscr{G}$ reen Pea Salad

2 pounds fresh green peas, shelled **Mayonnaise**
4 green onions   **Butter lettuce**

■ In a saucepan cook the peas in boiling salted water until tender. Immediately drain and place under cold running water. Refrigerate until chilled.

Thinly slice the green onions, including some tops. In a mixing bowl combine the peas and onions. Add enough mayonnaise to make a salad dressing.

Arrange the leaves of the butter lettuce to form cups. Spoon salad into them.

Makes 4 servings.

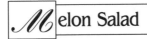elon Salad

2 cantaloupes	1 pint fresh blueberries
2 honeydew melons	Mint sprigs
1 medium watermelon	

■ Cut each of the cantaloupes, honeydew, and watermelons in half. Discard the seeds. Scoop out the centers using a melon ball cutter. Place the melon balls in a large salad bowl. Toss with blueberries. Garnish with mint sprigs.

Makes 12 servings.

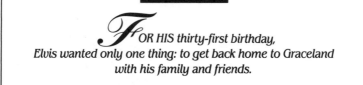

*OR HIS thirty-first birthday,
Elvis wanted only one thing: to get back home to Graceland
with his family and friends.*

each Aspic

1 ¼-ounce envelope unflavored gelatin	Grated rind of 1 lemon
1½ cups water	2 tablespoons fresh lemon juice
2 3-ounce packages peach gelatin	1½ cups peeled, pitted, and mashed peaches
1 cup orange juice	¼ cup sugar

Cream Cheese Dressing

1 3-ounce package cream cheese, softened	1 peach, peeled, pitted, and mashed
1 tablespoon mayonnaise	

■ In a small bowl soften the unflavored gelatin in ¼ cup of cold water. Stir to dissolve. In a saucepan bring 1¼ cups of water to a boil. Add the peach gelatin, and stir to dissolve. Add the unflavored gelatin, stirring well. Add the orange juice, lemon rind, lemon juice, mashed peaches, and sugar. Pour the mixture into a ring mold. Refrigerate until set.

In a small bowl beat the cream cheese until smooth. Add the mayonnaise and mashed peach, and blend well. Unmold the peach aspic and fill the center with the Cream Cheese Dressing.

Makes 6 servings.

Fit For a King

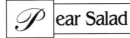

$\mathscr{P}$ ear Salad

1 3-ounce package lime gelatin	Salt to taste
1 cup hot water	Ginger to taste
1 cup pear juice	2 pears, peeled, cored, and diced
1 tablespoon vinegar	Shredded lettuce

■ Dissolve the gelatin in the hot water. Add the pear juice, vinegar, salt, and ginger. Refrigerate. When somewhat thickened, fold in the diced pears.

Turn the salad into a 4-cup mold. Refrigerate until completely thickened. Unmold onto a bed of shredded lettuce.

Makes 6 servings.

☆ ELVIS at the front door of Graceland

 idney Bean Salad

1 15-ounce can kidney beans, drained	¼ cup sweet pickle relish
	½ teaspoon salt
1 cup chopped celery	⅛ teaspoon chili powder
1 tablespoon chopped onion	½ teaspoon mustard

■ In a salad bowl combine the celery, onion, and pickle relish. Blend in the seasonings. Add the kidney beans and toss thoroughly. Refrigerate until chilled.

Makes 4 servings.

F HE EVER felt a prisoner of his fame, Elvis never showed it. He always considered himself the shy, quiet type who preferred being at home with his family and friends.

aked Apples

4 baking apples	4 teaspoons butter
½ cup packed light brown sugar	

■ Cut the apples in half and core. Do not peel. Place the apples in a deep baking dish, skin-side down. Sprinkle water around the base of each apple. Inside each apple spoon 1 tablespoon of brown sugar and ½ teaspoon of butter.

Bake at 350° for about 35 minutes or until the apples are tender. Baste once during the baking process.

Makes 4 servings.

Fit For a King

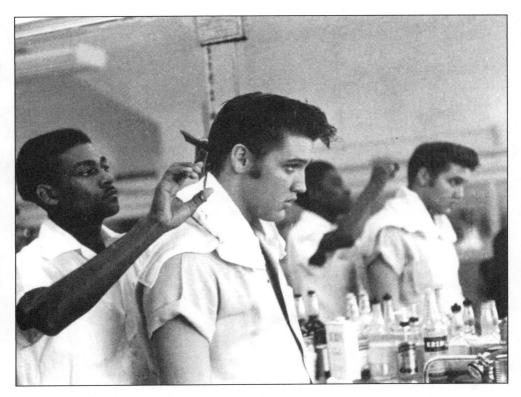

☆ **ELVIS'S hair was just one element in his natural good looks; here he is getting it styled.**

WHEN asked how he felt about his lifestyle change after being drafted into the army, Elvis said, "I certainly don't mind the hard work. I've done plenty of it before this. Everybody keeps asking me what I'll do in the army. I'm going into the service and do the best I can. If they want me to sing, I'll sing. If they want me to march—anything they want me to do is all right—whatever it is. I won't ask for special favors.

"The oddity is to get up and start running before breakfast. Breakfast is the one meal I count on. But the army isn't so rough. My folks had it rough. We lived in a housing project, and we were used to a hard life."

$\mathscr{S}$pinach Salad

4 hard-boiled eggs	1 cup diced celery
1½ pound fresh spinach, cleaned and chopped	¾ cup mayonnaise
	¼ teaspoon salt
¼ cup minced onion	1 teaspoon vinegar
1 cup diced sharp Cheddar cheese	Tabasco to taste

■ Remove and reserve the yolks from the eggs. Chop the egg whites. In a salad bowl toss the chopped egg whites with the remaining ingredients. Crumble the reserved egg yolks, and sprinkle them over the salad.

Makes 6 servings.

$\mathscr{E}$LVIS *always considered Graceland and Memphis his home. His friends and family were there: people he grew up with, went to church and school with. He never thought of leaving and only lived in Hollywood while he was working. He never considered moving there permanently.*

$\mathscr{C}$hicken Salad

½ cup chicken fat	3 cups diced cooked chicken
½ cup vinegar	2 cups diced celery
½ teaspoon onion juice	¼ cup capers
Salt and pepper to taste	Mayonnaise

■ In a mixing bowl blend the chicken fat, vinegar, onion juice, salt, and pepper. Pour over the diced chicken. Let the chicken marinate for about 2 hours.

Drain the chicken. In a salad bowl blend the chicken with the celery, capers, and desired amount of mayonnaise. Refrigerate until chilled.

Makes 6 servings.

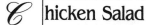

Fit For a King

una Salad

1 7-ounce can tuna, drained	¾ cup diced celery
1 tablespoon fresh lemon juice	1 hard-boiled egg, diced
¼ teaspoon onion juice	⅓ cup mayonnaise
Tabasco sauce to taste	1 cup shredded lettuce

■ In a mixing bowl blend the tuna with the lemon juice. Add the onion juice, Tabasco, celery, and egg. Toss lightly. Add the mayonnaise and blend thoroughly. Refrigerate for about 30 minutes. Serve on beds of shredded lettuce.

Makes 2 servings.

tuffed Tomatoes

5 medium tomatoes	1 tablespoon finely chopped onion
1 cup diced celery	Salt and pepper to taste
1 cucumber, peeled and diced	⅓ cup mayonnaise

■ Wash the tomatoes. Cut out the stems. Scoop out and reserve the centers. Refrigerate the tomatoes while preparing the filling.

In a mixing bowl combine the reserved tomato, celery, cucumbers, onions, salt, and pepper. Toss lightly. Add the mayonnaise. Stuff the chilled tomatoes with the filling.

Makes 5 servings.

$\mathscr{S}$IDE $\mathscr{D}$ISHES

$\mathscr{A}$ sparagus Casserole

1 teaspoon olive oil
1 medium onion, chopped
1 large clove garlic, peeled
4 cups asparagus tips
1 8-ounce package egg noodles

¾ cup heavy cream
½ cup grated Swiss cheese
Salt and pepper to taste
¼ cup grated Parmesan cheese

■ In a heavy saucepan heat the olive oil and sauté the onions. Add the garlic, and sauté for 1 minute. Remove the garlic. Add the asparagus and water to cover. Cover the pan and steam the asparagus until tender. Add water if needed.

Cook the egg noodles according to the package directions. Drain.

Drain the asparagus. In a casserole dish combine the asparagus, cream, Swiss cheese, salt, and pepper. Fold in the egg noodles. Sprinkle with Parmesan cheese.

Makes 4 servings.

$\mathscr{N}$OTHING made Elvis happier than
seeing his mother and father getting in for free at Loew's Theater,
where he ushered for $12.50 a week. He loved to watch them as they
enjoyed the movie. He particularly liked it when they would
share a tub of popcorn or a candy bar.

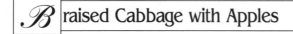# $\mathscr{B}$raised Cabbage with Apples

1 pound cooking apples	**¼ teaspoon cloves**
2 pounds red cabbage	**3 tablespoons light brown sugar**
1 pound onions, chopped	**3 tablespoons white wine vinegar**
1 clove garlic, minced	**1½ teaspoons butter**
⅛ teaspoon nutmeg	**Salt and pepper to taste**
¼ teaspoon cinnamon	

■ Peel, core, and chop the apples. Discard the outer leaves of the cabbage. Cut the cabbage into quarters and remove the hard stalk. Shred the cabbage. In a large casserole dish layer part of the cabbage, chopped apples, and onions, and season with part of the garlic, nutmeg, cinnamon, cloves, and brown sugar. Continue to layer the ingredients, and sprinkle with garlic, spices, and sugar. Pour the vinegar over all, dot with butter, and season with salt and pepper. Cover the dish. Bake at 300° for about 2 hours and 30 minutes, stirring twice during baking.

Makes 6 servings.

# $\mathscr{M}$ashed Potatoes & Gravy

6 medium potatoes	**2 tablespoons butter**
½ cup hot milk	**Salt to taste**

Gravy

3 tablespoons fat	**1½ cups milk**
3 tablespoons all-purpose flour	**Salt and pepper to taste**
½ cup chicken stock	

■ Wash, peel, and thinly slice the potatoes. Bring a pot of salted water to a boil. Add the potato slices and boil until the potatoes are tender when pierced with a fork. Drain and return to the pot. Mash the potatoes with a fork. Add ½ cup of hot milk and butter. Beat with an electric mixer until light and fluffy. Add salt if needed. Heat through over low heat.

In a saucepan melt the fat and stir in the flour. When blended but not browned add the chicken stock and 1½ cups of milk. Stir constantly over low heat until smooth and thick. Season with salt and pepper.

Spoon the mashed potatoes into a heated serving dish. Top with the gravy.

Makes 6 servings.

☆ **TAKING time out from training to read a fan magazine**

WHEN asked if he was sorry to leave his career behind while stationed in the army, Elvis replied that he wasn't. "This will be a great time to catch my breath and relax a bit."

Although his outlook was a positive one, his fans on the other hand renamed March 24, 1958, the day he was inducted, Black Monday.

Did Elvis expect any special treatment? None whatsoever. He said that since he was an able-bodied American, he should serve his country like everyone else.

Side Dishes

☆ **SPORTING shorter sideburns while in the army**

Tomato Fritters

2 medium tomatoes
½ cup plus 2 tablespoons all-
   purpose flour
½ teaspoon sugar
½ teaspoon baking powder

1 egg, beaten
¼ teaspoon Worcestershire sauce
¾ cup Gruyere
Oil for deep frying

■ Bring a large saucepan of water to boil. Plunge the tomatoes in the water, and hold them there for about 1 minute. Remove the tomatoes from the water and hold them under cold running water to remove the skins. Cut the tomatoes horizontally, and remove the seeds. Coarsely chop the tomatoes.

In a mixing bowl combine the flour, sugar, and baking powder. Add the beaten egg, tomatoes, Worcestershire sauce, and cheese, stirring to coat the tomatoes. Shape the mixture into patties or balls, and deep fry in hot oil for about 30 seconds on each side or until golden. Drain on paper towels.

Makes 4 servings.

Fit For a King

ℬ lack Bean Chili

2 cups dry black beans
2 tablespoons cumin seed
2 tablespoons dried oregano
   leaves
2 large onions, chopped
1½ green bell peppers, diced
3 tablespoons minced garlic

½ cup olive oil
4½ teaspoons paprika
½ teaspoon salt
2 8-ounce cans crushed tomatoes
3 jalapeño peppers, seeded,
   deveined, and chopped

■ In a large saucepan boil the beans. Remove the beans from the heat and let them stand for about 2 hours. Drain. Add fresh water to the pan to cover the beans plus 2 inches. Bring the water to a boil, reduce the heat, and simmer for about 2 hours. Drain and reserve the liquid.

On a baking sheet spread out the cumin seeds and oregano leaves. Bake at 325° for about 10 minutes, shaking the pan regularly.

In a frying pan heat the olive oil and sauté the vegetables for about 3 minutes. Add the baked cumin seeds and oregano leaves, as well as the paprika and salt. Sauté for about 8 minutes. Add the vegetables to the pot and bring the mixture to a simmer. Add the reserved liquid as needed. Simmer for about 30 minutes.

Makes 8 cups.

ℭ arolina Sweet Potatoes

3 cups cooked and mashed sweet
   potatoes
1 cup sugar
2 eggs

½ cup butter, melted
1 teaspoon vanilla extract
½ cup milk

Topping
1 cup packed light brown sugar
½ cup self-rising flour

5½ teaspoons butter
1 cup chopped pecans

■ In a mixing bowl combine the potatoes, sugar, eggs, ½ cup of butter, vanilla, and milk. Grease a 9-inch baking pan. Transfer the potato mixture to the prepared pan.

In a separate bowl combine the brown sugar, flour, butter, and pecans, mixing well. Sprinkle the mixture over the potatoes. Bake at 350° for about 30 minutes.

Makes 6 servings.

☆ **WITH Vernon and Gladys before leaving for Killeen, Texas**

$\mathcal{G}$ rilled Zucchini

1 pound zucchini, sliced ¼-inch
   thick
1 tablespoon olive oi!
1 tablespoon grated Parmesan
   cheese

2 cups grated Mozzarella cheese
Salt and pepper to taste
½ teaspoon oregano

■ Brush the zucchini with olive oil and arrange the zucchini slices in a baking pan. Sprinkle with Parmesan cheese, Mozzarella, salt, pepper, and oregano. Broil for about 5 minutes.

   Makes 6 servings.

Fit For a King

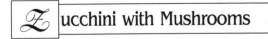ucchini with Mushrooms

1 pound zucchini, peeled
1 large red bell pepper
1 cup mushrooms
½ cup olive oil
¼ cup minced shallots

3 tablespoons red wine vinegar
½ teaspoon sugar
Salt and pepper to taste
¼ cup chopped parsley

■ Cut the zucchini diagonally into ¼-inch slices. Cut the red bell peppers and mushrooms into ½-inch pieces.

In a serving bowl whisk together the olive oil, shallots, vinegar, sugar, salt, and pepper. Add the zucchini, mushrooms, red bell pepper, and parsley, and toss thoroughly. Cover and refrigerate for about 3 hours.

Makes 6 servings.

E LVIS spoke with the press after the death of his mother, Gladys. "She was the most wonderful mother in the world. And she was so young to die. I will think of her every day."

Creamed Zucchini

5 zucchini, peeled and chopped
½ cup grated Parmesan cheese
**1 8-ounce package cream cheese,
   softened**

Salt and pepper to taste
3 tablespoons bread crumbs

■ In a saucepan cover the zucchini with water and boil until tender. Drain. Add the Parmesan and cream cheese. Mash the mixture with a fork. Season with salt and pepper. Transfer the zucchini to a 2-quart casserole dish. Sprinkle the bread crumbs over the top. Bake at 350° for about 10 minutes.

Makes 4 to 6 servings.

Side Dishes

ucchini with Parmesan Cheese

4 cups peeled and sliced zucchini
2 cups water
1 cup mayonnaise
1 medium onion, chopped

1 cup grated Parmesan cheese
¼ cup chopped green bell pepper
2 eggs, beaten

■ In a saucepan boil the zucchini in the water. Drain. In a mixing bowl combine the remaining ingredients. Add the zucchini and mix thoroughly.

Grease a 1½-quart baking dish. Transfer the zucchini mixture to the prepared dish. Bake at 350° for about 40 minutes or until golden brown. Cool for about 5 minutes. Slice into 2-inch squares before serving.

Makes 6 servings.

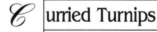 urried Turnips

¼ cup oil
4 turnips, peeled and cut into
**   1-inch cubes**
1½ teaspoons cumin seeds
1 tablespoon sesame seeds
¼ cup peeled and ground roasted
**   peanuts**
1 onion, sliced

½ teaspoon cayenne pepper
½ teaspoon turmeric
½ teaspoon salt
1 teaspoon packed light brown
**   sugar**
Juice of ½ lemon
1½ cups water
Pinch lemon rind

■ In a heavy saucepan heat the oil. Fry the turnips for about 5 minutes. Remove the turnips from the skillet and set aside. In the same oil sauté the cumin seeds. When slightly browned add the sesame seeds, peanuts, and onion slices. Be careful not to scorch the spices.

Sauté the onion slices until golden. Add the cayenne pepper, turmeric, and salt, and fry for about 5 minutes over low heat. Add the turnips, sugar, lemon juice, water, and a pinch of lemon rind. Cook uncovered until the turnips are soft.

Makes 6 servings.

ℬ utternut Squash & Shrimp

1 medium butternut squash	**1 small clove garlic, minced**
Salt to taste	**1 cup peeled and deveined shrimp**
¼ cup oil	**1 cup water**
1 small onion, sliced	

■ Cut the butternut squash into 1-inch cubes. Remove the seeds but do not peel off the skin. Season with salt. Set aside.

In a saucepan heat the oil. Sauté the onions with the garlic until soft. Add the seasoned squash and the shrimp. Pour in the water, and simmer until the squash is tender. Add additional water if necessary.

Makes 4 servings.

𝒞 urried Rice Salad

2 cups white rice, cooked and	**2 tablespoons raisins**
chilled	**2 tablespoons chopped parsley**
1 green bell pepper, chopped	**2 tablespoons chopped green onion**
4 teaspoons pimiento, cut and	
drained	

Dressing

½ cup olive oil	**½ teaspoon curry powder**
⅓ cup red wine vinegar	**Salt and pepper to taste**
1 clove garlic, minced	**1 tablespoon fresh lemon juice**
1 tablespoon sugar	

■ In a large salad bowl combine the rice, bell pepper, pimiento, raisins, parsley, and green onion. Toss well and refrigerate.

In a separate bowl blend the olive oil with the vinegar. Add the garlic, sugar, curry powder, salt, and pepper. Blend in the lemon juice. Toss the dressing into the salad.

Makes 6 servings.

Side Dishes

☆ **ELVIS, who usually drank milk, taking time out for tea**

ucchini & Yellow Squash

1 pound zucchini	1 teaspoon salt
1 pound summer squash	¼ teaspoon white pepper
1 tablespoon butter	1 tablespoon chives

■ Cut the zucchini and yellow squash lengthwise. Cut each piece in half. Scoop out the seeds and shred with the coarse side of a grater.

In a skillet melt the butter. Add the zucchini, squash, salt, and pepper. Sauté the mixture, stirring constantly, for about 5 minutes. Add the chives and serve.

Makes 6 servings.

Fit For a King

𝓜ushrooms with Spinach

1 16-ounce package egg noodles	1 pound mushrooms, sliced
¼ cup butter	1 cup vegetable stock
1 onion, chopped	8 cups torn fresh spinach
3 cloves garlic, minced	1½ cups sour cream
1½ teaspoons paprika	1 teaspoon Worcestershire sauce
¼ teaspoon nutmeg	½ teaspoon Tabasco sauce

■ Cook the egg noodles according to the package directions. Drain. In a saucepan melt the butter and sauté the onions, garlic, paprika, and nutmeg. Add the mushrooms and sauté until the liquid evaporates.

Add the vegetable stock and bring the mixture to a boil. Boil until the liquid is reduced by half. Add the spinach, sour cream, Worcestershire sauce, and Tabasco. Serve over the cooked egg noodles.

Makes 6 servings.

𝓢callops in Cream Sauce

2 tablespoons butter	1 cup dry white wine
1 small leek, julienned	½ teaspoon salt
1 carrot, julienned	White pepper to taste
1 rib celery, julienned	1 cup heavy cream
2 tablespoons minced shallots	3 egg yolks
2 pounds sea scallops	1 teaspoon fresh lemon juice

■ In a saucepan melt 1 tablespoon of butter. Add the leeks, carrots, and celery, and sauté until tender. Remove the vegetables. Add remaining butter and shallots, and sauté until transparent. Add the scallops, wine, salt, and pepper. Increase the heat and sauté for about 4 minutes, turning the scallops gently. Remove the scallops and boil the liquid until reduced by half. Reserve the liquid.

In a mixing bowl beat the cream with the egg yolks. Slowly add the reserved liquid. Stir until thickened. Blend in the lemon juice. Add the scallops and ¾ of the vegetables. Stir until thoroughly heated. Garnish with the remaining vegetables.

Makes 6 servings.

Side Dishes

orn Pudding

3 eggs
1 cup milk
1 tablespoon sugar
1 teaspoon salt
2 cups cream-style corn

2 tablespoons all-purpose flour
1 tablespoon minced onion
¼ cup minced green bell pepper
1 tablespoon butter

■ In a mixing bowl beat the eggs lightly. Add the milk, sugar, and salt, and blend well. Add the corn and remaining ingredients. Transfer the batter to a casserole dish. Bake uncovered at 350° for about 1 hour.

Makes 6 servings.

 lazed Carrots

6 carrots, sliced ¼-inch thick
¼ cup fresh orange juice
1 tablespoon unsalted butter
¼ teaspoon ginger

1 tablespoon packed light brown
  sugar
1 tablespoon sugar

■ In a skillet combine carrots, orange juice, butter, ginger, brown sugar, and sugar. Bring the liquid to a boil and reduce the heat to a simmer. Cover and cook until the carrots are somewhat tender.

Uncover and return the liquid to a boil. Cook until most of the liquid has evaporated.
Makes 2 servings.

aked Beans

2 pounds dried navy beans
2 quarts cold water
1 medium onion, sliced
1½ teaspoons salt
¼ cup apple cider vinegar
1 teaspoon mustard

2 tablespoons packed light brown
  sugar
½ cup molasses
¼ cup ketchup
Black pepper to taste
½ pound salted pork, sliced

- Wash the beans thoroughly. Place the beans in a saucepan with cold water, cover and heat to boiling. Simmer for about 30 minutes. Drain and reserve the liquid. Place the onion slices in a 10-inch casserole dish. Add the salt, vinegar, mustard, brown sugar, molasses, ketchup, and pepper. Add the beans and 2½ cups of the reserved liquid. Arrange the salt pork slices on the top. Cover. Bake at 250° for about 7 to 8 hours.

Halfway through baking, remove 2 cups of beans and mash them thoroughly. Blend the mashed beans into the remaining beans. Cover and continue baking. Add water as needed. The beans should be covered with a thick liquid. Remove the cover 1 hour before the beans are done.

Makes 10 servings.

ELVIS'S friend, Elaine Owens, remembered the warmth and hospitality offered to her when she visited him in Killeen, Texas. She spoke of how Gladys invited her to stay for dinner. Gladys had prepared a southern feast with a ham and a big pot of baked beans. For dessert she served them a fresh baked cake with ice cream. After supper, they were joined by two of Elvis's friends and a cousin. They sat around the living room and put on a private show for their guest. Elvis, who played the piano, had everyone join in with the singing.

Curried Shrimp & Scallops

½ cup clarified butter
2 tablespoons curry powder
½ pound sea scallops, cut into chunks

¼ pound shrimp, shelled and deveined
1 cup light cream
1 fresh lemon

- In a skillet melt enough clarified butter to cover the bottom of the pan. Add the curry powder. Cook about 2 minutes or until the powder turns dark. Add the scallops and shrimp. Cook until the shrimp begins turning pink. Reduce the heat to low. Add the cream. Cut 5 thin slices from the lemon. Squeeze the juice from the remaining lemon slowly into the curry. Cover with the lemon slices.

Makes 6 servings.

Side Dishes

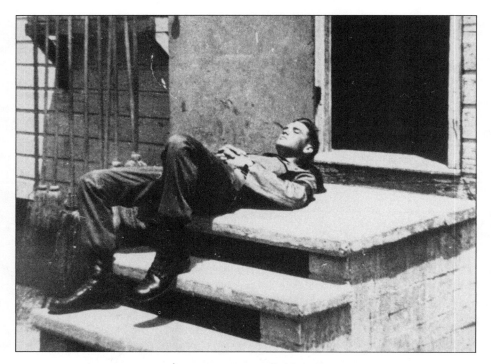

☆ TAKING a break from training

*M*ustard Greens & Potatoes

⅛ pound salt pork
6 cups cold water
4 cups mustard greens

12 new potatoes
Salt and pepper to taste

■ Thinly slice the salt pork and place it in a pan. Add the cold water, cover, and simmer for about 60 minutes. Wash and clean the mustard greens. Wash and peel the potatoes. Add the stalks of the mustard greens to the steamed pork, and cook for about 15 minutes.

Add the potatoes and the tops of the mustard greens. Cook for about 15 minutes more. Season with salt and pepper.

Makes 6 servings.

Fit For a King

$\mathscr{C}$orn Bread Stuffing

½ pound pork sausage links, sliced ½-inch thick	4 cups cubed stale bread
¼ cup butter	¼ teaspoon salt
½ pound mushrooms, sliced	¼ cup chopped parsley
1 medium onion, sliced	2 tablespoons marjoram
1 cup diced celery	1 tablespoon sage
4 cups crumbled corn bread	½ cup chicken broth

■ In a large skillet fry the sausage over medium heat. Cook until the pink color has disappeared. Spoon off and discard most of the fat. Add the butter, mushrooms, onion, and celery. Cook until the vegetables are soft and the sausage and mushrooms are slightly browned.

In a large mixing bowl combine the corn bread and cubed bread. Add the sausage, vegetables, and seasonings. Mix to toss. Add the chicken broth. Toss just until the bread is moistened, and stuff a cooked turkey.

Place any leftover stuffing in a buttered casserole dish. Cover and bake at 350° for about 35 minutes.

Makes enough to stuff a 15-pound turkey.

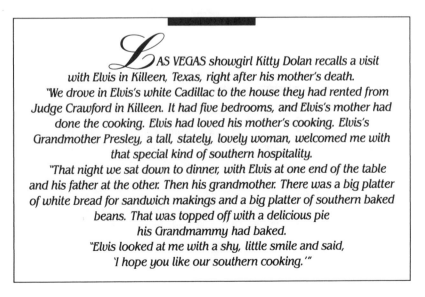

$\mathscr{L}$AS VEGAS showgirl Kitty Dolan recalls a visit with Elvis in Killeen, Texas, right after his mother's death. "We drove in Elvis's white Cadillac to the house they had rented from Judge Crawford in Killeen. It had five bedrooms, and Elvis's mother had done the cooking. Elvis had loved his mother's cooking. Elvis's Grandmother Presley, a tall, stately, lovely woman, welcomed me with that special kind of southern hospitality.

"That night we sat down to dinner, with Elvis at one end of the table and his father at the other. Then his grandmother. There was a big platter of white bread for sandwich makings and a big platter of southern baked beans. That was topped off with a delicious pie his Grandmammy had baked.

"Elvis looked at me with a shy, little smile and said, 'I hope you like our southern cooking.'"

☆ **ELVIS being greeted by fans in Germany**

WHEN Elvis was asked why he didn't date seriously while stationed in Germany, he answered that although he had met a lot of people and made a lot of new friends, marriage was "serious business."
He didn't feel that language was a barrier, nor was the geography. His only concern was that he had made no plans to marry. But when he did meet the right girl, he would settle down for keeps.

$\mathscr{C}$ harleston Red Rice

2 cups raw long-grain rice	1 8-ounce can tomato sauce
4 cups water	1 6-ounce can tomato paste
3 teaspoons salt	3 teaspoons sugar
6 slices bacon	2 teaspoons Worcestershire sauce
2 medium onions, finely chopped	Red pepper sauce to taste

■ In a saucepan cook the rice in boiling salted water until light and fluffy. In a skillet fry the bacon until crisp. Drain on paper towels.

Sauté the chopped onions in 4 tablespoons of the bacon fat, until they become transparent. Add the tomato sauce, tomato paste, sugar, Worcestershire sauce, and red pepper sauce. Cook slowly for about 10 minutes. Add the tomato mixture to the rice.

Place the cooked rice in a greased 2-quart baking dish. In a bowl blend the seasonings together, and add them to the rice. Bake at 325° for about 45 minutes or until the rice has absorbed all of the liquid. Crumble the bacon over the top.

Makes 12 servings.

$\mathscr{W}$ ild Rice with Mushrooms

1 cup wild rice, washed	3 tablespoons butter
2 cups cold water	1 tablespoon minced onion
¼ teaspoon salt	¼ pound fresh mushrooms, sliced

■ In a saucepan combine the wild rice, water, and salt. Cover and cook until the rice is tender. In a skillet melt the butter. Sauté the onions with the mushrooms for about 5 minutes.

In a casserole dish toss the mushrooms and onion into the wild rice.

Makes 4 servings.

$\mathcal{S}$ pinach & Rice Casserole

1 10-ounce package frozen chopped spinach	3 cups cooked white rice ½ cup shredded Cheddar cheese
¼ cup butter	2 eggs
1 cup sliced mushrooms	1 12-ounce can evaporated milk
½ cup chopped onion	1 tablespoon water
1 clove garlic, minced	Salt and pepper to taste

■ Prepare the spinach according to the package directions. Drain well. In a saucepan melt the butter and sauté the mushrooms, onion, and garlic until tender. In a large bowl combine the mushroom mixture, spinach, rice, and Cheddar cheese. Transfer the mixture to a casserole dish.

In a separate saucepan heat together the eggs, milk, water, salt, and pepper. Pour the liquid over the spinach mixture and mix well. Bake at 350° for about 30 minutes.

Makes 4 servings.

$\mathcal{L}$IKE many young girls her age, Priscilla Beaulieu was dying to meet Elvis Presley. Her first "date" with Elvis was while he was stationed in Germany. She went to his house for a home-cooked southern supper prepared by Elvis's grandmother, Minnie Presley.

$\mathcal{M}$ ustard Greens

½ pound salt pork	2 bunches mustard greens, washed
1 onion, chopped	and stemmed
Salt and pepper to taste	

■ In a casserole dish combine the salt pork, onion, and seasonings with the mustard greens. Add no water. Cover and cook slowly until the pork and mustard greens are tender.

Makes 4 servings.

☆ WITH his father, Vernon

$\mathcal{P}$ an-Fried Potatoes & Gravy

¼ cup butter   Salt and pepper to taste
6 medium new potatoes, sliced

Gravy
1 tablespoon butter   1 cup milk
1 tablespoon all-purpose flour   Salt and pepper to taste

■ In a skillet melt ¼ cup of butter. Add the sliced potatoes. Season with salt and pepper. Cook over medium heat until golden, turning constantly. Remove the potatoes to a heated platter. In the skillet combine the ingredients for the gravy. Stir until somewhat thickened. Pour the gravy over the potatoes.
    Makes 4 servings.

Side Dishes

𝒞 ranberry Squash

1 pound raw winter squash, peeled and cut into 1-inch cubes	**2 tablespoons raisins**
½ cup fresh cranberries	**Juice and rind from 1 small orange**
1 small apple, chopped into ½-inch slices	**1 tablespoon honey**
	1 tablespoon butter, melted
	Salt to taste

■ In a baking dish arrange the squash in a single layer on the bottom. Scatter the cranberries, apples, and raisins over the top. Add the remaining ingredients and toss to coat. Cover. Bake at 400° for about 30 minutes or until the squash is tender.

Makes 6 servings.

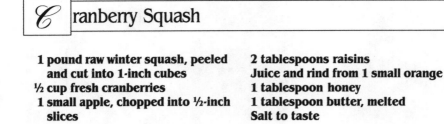

𝒰PON Elvis's return to the United States, family and friends threw him a big welcome home party at Graceland. Fans gathered at the gates to catch a glimpse of Elvis as his car made its way up the driveway. Inside, Grandmother Presley had baked a special cake for the occasion.

𝒮 quash Supreme

2 pounds summer squash, cooked	**1 cup sour cream**
1 10¾-ounce can cream of chicken soup	**1 teaspoon salt**
2 tablespoons minced onion	**Pepper to taste**
1 carrot, grated	**1 8-ounce package seasoned bread crumbs**

■ In a bowl mash the squash. Add the soup, onion, carrot, sour cream, salt, and pepper. Butter a 2-quart casserole dish. Sprinkle a layer of the seasoned bread crumbs in the bottom. Add the squash mixture. Cover with the remaining crumbs. Dot with butter. Bake at 350° about 30 minutes.

Makes 5 servings.

$\mathscr{S}$ pinach & Artichoke Casserole

1 14-ounce can non-marinated artichoke hearts	2 tablespoons mayonnaise
3 10-ounce packages frozen, chopped spinach	6 tablespoons milk
1 8-ounce package cream cheese, softened	Freshly ground pepper to taste
	Grated Parmesan cheese to taste

■ Cut the artichoke hearts in half and place them in a casserole dish. Cover with the spinach.

In a mixing bowl combine the cream cheese, mayonnaise, and milk. Spread over the spinach. Sprinkle with pepper and Parmesan cheese. Bake at 375° for about 35 to 40 minutes.

Makes 6 servings.

☆ **SHOWING** off his dog tags

Side Dishes

 calloped Oysters

2 cups oysters	**1 cup cracker crumbs**
4 tablespoons oyster juice	**½ cup butter, melted**
2 tablespoons light cream	**Salt and pepper to taste**
½ cup stale bread crumbs	

■ In a casserole dish combine all of the ingredients. Mix thoroughly. Bake at 450° for about 30 minutes.

Makes 4 servings.

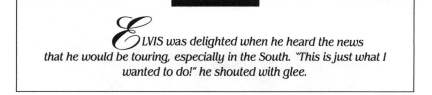

LVIS was delighted when he heard the news that he would be touring, especially in the South. "This is just what I wanted to do!" he shouted with glee.

 calloped Eggplant

1 large eggplant, peeled and sliced	**1 10¾-ounce can cream of mushroom soup**
1 small onion, chopped	**1 egg, beaten**
2 tablespoons butter	**⅓ cup soft bread crumbs**
1 teaspoon sugar	**3 tablespoons grated Parmesan**
1 tablespoon Worcestershire sauce	**cheese**

■ Soak the eggplant in salted water for about 30 minutes. Drain. Drop the eggplant into boiling water and cook until tender. In a saucepan melt the butter and sauté the onion until transparent.

In a mixing bowl combine the onion, eggplant, sugar, Worcestershire sauce, soup, and egg. Pour the mixture into a 2-quart buttered casserole dish. Sprinkle with bread crumbs and Parmesan cheese. Bake at 350° for about 40 minutes.

Makes 6 servings.

Fit For a King

☆ ELVIS at center stage in concert

$\mathscr{S}$ piced Potatoes

1½ pounds small new potatoes,
    scrubbed
2 tablespoons oil
6 tablespoons sesame seeds
1 tablespoon mustard seed

1 inch fresh ginger root, peeled and
    grated
½ teaspoon chili powder
2 teaspoons fresh lemon juice
Salt to taste

■ In a saucepan boil the potatoes until tender and drain. In a skillet heat the oil. Add the sesame seeds, mustard seed, ginger, chili powder, and salt.

Cook over a moderate heat about 4 minutes. Add the potatoes and stir. Add the lemon juice. Refrigerate overnight. Serve cold.

Makes 4 cups.

Side Dishes

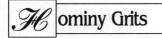 ried Okra

1 pound young okra	**Pepper to taste**
½ cup cornmeal	**Dash cayenne pepper**
¼ teaspoon salt	

■ Cut off the stems and the tips of the okra pods. Wash thoroughly and place them in a pan of boiling salted water. Cook for about 8 minutes. Drain and let dry thoroughly.

In a mixing bowl blend the cornmeal with the salt, pepper, and cayenne pepper. Roll the okra in the seasoned cornmeal. Fry in deep fat (350°) or sauté in butter until brown.

Makes 6 servings.

 ominy Grits

1 cup hominy grits	**2 teaspoons salt**
5 cups water	

■ In the top of a double boiler over simmering water bring the 5 cups of water and the salt to a boil. Add the hominy grits. Boil for about 10 minutes over direct heat. Then remove to the lower portion of the double boiler. Continue cooking for about 2 hours.

Makes 4 servings.

ash Brown Potatoes

3 large potatoes	**Pepper to taste**
2 tablespoons grated onions	**⅓ cup butter**
1 teaspoon salt	

■ Bake the potatoes with skins. Let cool thoroughly. Once cooled, peel and thinly slice to make 4 cups. Toss with the grated onion, and season with salt and pepper.

In a skillet melt the butter. Brown the potatoes in the butter for about 10 minutes. Reduce the heat and continue cooking for about 8 minutes or until golden brown.

Makes 4 servings.

Fit For a King

$\mathscr{C}$ urried Cauliflower

2 tablespoons sesame seeds
2 tablespoons cumin seeds
½ cup grated unsweetened
  coconut
½ teaspoon cloves
2 cloves garlic
1½ teaspoons grated fresh ginger
  root

½ teaspoon turmeric
¼ teaspoon cayenne pepper
3 tablespoons butter
1½ cups chopped onion
1 medium cauliflower, broken into
  flowerettes
½ teaspoon salt
Juice of ½ lemon

■ In a saucepan heat the sesame and cumin seeds over medium-high heat. Shake occasionally until they become fragrant and begin to pop. In a blender purée the coconut, cloves, garlic, ginger, turmeric, and cayenne pepper with the sesame and cumin seeds. Add enough water to make a thick paste. In a saucepan melt the butter and sauté the onions. Add the cauliflower, salt, and the paste mixture. Mix thoroughly and reduce the heat to low. Simmer, stirring occasionally, until the cauliflower is tender. Blend in the lemon juice. Turn off the heat and let the cauliflower sit for 5 minutes.
  Makes 4 servings.

$\mathscr{C}$ heese Grits

4 cups boiling water
1 teaspoon salt
1 cup instant grits
½ cup butter

1 6-ounce roll garlic cheese
2 eggs
Milk

■ Bring a pan of salted water to a boil. Slowly stir in the grits. Cook for about 3 minutes, stirring constantly. Remove from the heat. Add the butter and garlic cheese.
  In a measuring cup mix the eggs with the milk to make 1 cup. Beat well and add to the grits mixture. Transfer the grits to a greased 2-quart casserole dish. Bake at 300° for about 1 hour.
  Makes 6 servings.

Side Dishes

☆ **POSING for the March of Dimes in 1957**

BREADS

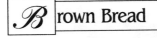

Brown Bread

1½ cups all-purpose flour
1½ teaspoons baking soda
1 teaspoon salt

1 cup whole-wheat flour
1½ cups butter
Milk

■ Into a mixing bowl sift together the all-purpose flour, baking soda, and salt. Stir in the whole wheat flour. Cut in the butter with a pastry blender. Gradually add the milk until the batter consists of a soft dough. Turn the dough onto a floured board and knead. Shape the bread into a loaf and place it in a floured loaf pan. Bake at 425° for about 30 minutes or until brown.

Makes 1 loaf.

Buttermilk Bread

3 envelopes active dry yeast
¾ cup very hot water
¼ cup sugar
¼ cup butter

2 cups buttermilk, scalded
3 teaspoons salt
½ teaspoon baking soda
5½ cups sifted all-purpose flour

■ In a small bowl combine the yeast and water, and stir until dissolved. In a large bowl combine the remaining ingredients, and add the dissolved yeast. Knead the mixture into a dough. Cover and let the dough rise until doubled in bulk.

Separate the dough into 2 loaves. Place the loaves in lightly greased loaf pans and let them rise again. Bake at 400° for 40 to 50 minutes. Cool before serving.

Makes 2 loaves.

# $\mathscr{S}$hortbread

1 cup butter	**½ cup cornstarch**
1 cup all-purpose flour	**½ cup sugar**

■ In a saucepan melt the butter. In a bowl mix the flour, cornstarch, and ¼ cup sugar. Add the melted butter to the dry ingredients and mix thoroughly. Press the mixture into an 8-inch square baking pan, using the back of a spoon to level. Prick with a fork 2 to 3 times.

Bake at 325° for about 35 minutes. Sprinkle sugar over the top. Cut into squares. Remove from the pan when cooled.

Makes 9 squares.

☆ **WITH his date at the Roller Rink in Memphis**

Fit For a King

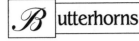utterhorns

2 envelopes active dry yeast
½ cup warm water (115°)
½ cup butter
⅔ cup sugar
3 eggs, beaten

1½ cups warm milk (115°)
8 cups all-purpose flour
1½ teaspoons salt
¼ cup butter, melted

■ In a small bowl combine the yeast and warm water, and set the mixture aside. In a separate bowl cream the butter with the sugar. Add the eggs, warm milk, and yeast. Add the flour and salt, a little at a time. Place the dough in a greased mixing bowl. Cover and refrigerate for about 3 hours.

Remove the dough from the refrigerator and let it stand for about 15 minutes. Turn the dough onto a floured board and knead lightly. Divide into 6 equal portions. Roll each into a circle about 9 inches in diameter. Cut each circle into 8 wedges. Brush with melted butter. Starting with the wider end of each wedge, roll up toward the point. Place the horns on an ungreased baking sheet. Let them rise for about 1 hour.

Bake at 350° for about 15 minutes.

Makes 48.

---

*F*AN MAGAZINE stories of "Girls Who Got to Elvis" tell variations of the same wholesome boy. Elvis splurged, but not on fancy restaurants or sophisticated nightclubs. He rented the Fairgrounds Amusement Park so he, his date, and his pals could ride Dodge-'Em cars. Or he might rent the Rainbow Roller Rink where they would play Crack-the-Whip and eat Pronto Pups dipped in mustard.

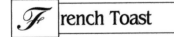rench Toast

1 egg
½ cup cold milk

4 slices bread
Butter

■ In a mixing bowl whip the egg with the milk. Dip the sliced bread into the batter. In a skillet melt enough butter to coat the bottom of the pan. Fry the dipped bread on both sides until browned.

Makes 4 servings.

Breads

*S*ourdough Starter

1 envelope active dry yeast
2 cups warm milk (115°)

2 cups all-purpose flour

■ In a 1½-quart glass jar combine the yeast, milk, and flour. Cover with a cheesecloth. Leave the batter in a warm room for about 48 hours, stirring 2 to 3 times. The batter should ferment, bubble, and acquire a slightly sour smell.

To use, stir and measure the amount needed for the recipe. Add equal parts of flour and milk to the remaining portion until it bubbles. Place the starter in a pressure seal container. Cover and refrigerate. Never add anything but flour and milk to the starter. To keep the starter active add equal amounts of flour and milk every two weeks. Keep the unused portion refrigerated.

Makes 3 cups.

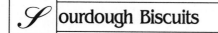

*S*ourdough Biscuits

1 cup whole-wheat flour
1 cup all-purpose flour
1 tablespoon sugar
1 teaspoon baking powder

½ teaspoon salt
½ cup butter
2 cups sourdough starter

■ In a mixing bowl sift together the flours, sugar, baking powder, and salt. With a pastry blender cut in the butter until the mixture is crumbly. Add 2 cups of sourdough starter and blend.

Turn the dough onto a floured board. Knead lightly. Cut into circles 2½ inches in diameter and place on a lightly oiled baking sheet. Let the biscuits rise in a warm place for about 30 minutes. Bake at 450° for about 20 to 25 minutes or until light brown.

Makes 2 dozen.

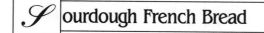

*S*ourdough French Bread

1½ cups warm water
1 cup sourdough starter
6 cups all-purpose flour

2 teaspoons sugar
1½ teaspoons salt
½ teaspoon baking soda

■ In a bowl mix the water and starter with 4 cups of flour, the salt, and sugar. Mix well. Place the dough in a greased mixing bowl and leave it at room temperature until doubled in size. Stir in 1 cup of the remaining flour and the baking soda.

Turn the dough onto a floured board. Knead, adding the remaining flour as needed. Knead for at least 8 minutes or until the dough cannot absorb any more flour. Shape into 2 oblong loaves or one round loaf. Place the loaves on a lightly greased baking sheet. Cover and let the loaves rise until nearly doubled in size. Just before baking, brush with water. Make diagonal slashes in the top with a sharp knife.

Place a shallow pan of water in the bottom of the oven. Brush the loaves with butter. Bake at 400° for about 45 minutes. The crust should become medium dark brown. Remove the loaves from the oven 10 minutes before they are done and brush with salted water. Return to the oven for the remaining time. Cool before serving.

Makes 2 oblong loaves or 1 round loaf.

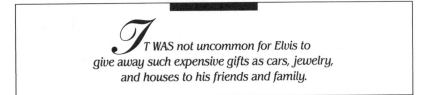

IT WAS not uncommon for Elvis to give away such expensive gifts as cars, jewelry, and houses to his friends and family.

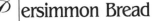ersimmon Bread

1 cup raisins	4 cups all-purpose flour
½ cup brandy	1 teaspoon baking soda
2 cups packed light brown sugar	¼ teaspoon salt
½ cup sugar	1 teaspoon cinnamon
2 cups ripe persimmon pulp	1 teaspoon nutmeg
1 cup oil	½ teaspoon ginger
4 eggs	1 cup chopped walnuts

■ In a small bowl plump the raisins in the brandy. In a large bowl combine the brown sugar, sugar, persimmon pulp, and oil. Add the eggs one at a time, beating well after each addition. Into a separate bowl sift together the dry ingredients. Fold the dry ingredients into the persimmon mixture, blending well. Add the plumped raisins and walnuts. Pour the batter into 4 buttered and floured 7-inch loaf pans. Bake at 350° for about 1 hour or until a tester inserted in the center comes out clean. Cool on a rack.

Makes 4 loaves.

Breads

☆ **A FAN taking advantage of a photo opportunity**

ℤucchini Bread

3 eggs	1 cup raisins
1 cup oil	1 cup chopped walnuts
1½ cups sugar	¼ teaspoon baking powder
2 teaspoons vanilla extract	2 teaspoons baking soda
2 cups peeled and grated zucchini	3 teaspoons cinnamon
2 cups all-purpose flour	½ teaspoon salt

■ In a large mixing bowl beat the eggs. Add the oil, sugar, vanilla, and zucchini. Add the remaining ingredients and blend thoroughly. Pour the batter into 2 loaf pans. Bake at 375° for about 1 hour. Let the bread cool before serving.

Makes 2 loaves.

Fit For a King

aspberry-Streusel Muffins

1½ cups all-purpose flour
¼ cup sugar
¼ cup packed light brown sugar
2 teaspoons baking powder
⅛ teaspoon salt
1 teaspoon cinnamon

1 egg, lightly beaten
½ cup unsalted butter, melted
½ cup milk
1¼ cups fresh raspberries
1 teaspoon grated lemon rind

Streusel Topping
½ cup chopped walnuts
½ cup packed light brown sugar
¼ cup all-purpose flour
1 teaspoon cinnamon

1 teaspoon grated lemon rind
2 tablespoons unsalted butter,
melted

Glaze
½ cup confectioners' sugar

1 tablespoon fresh lemon juice

■ Line 12 muffin cups with paper liners. Into a bowl sift together 1½ cups of flour, the sugar, ¼ cup of brown sugar, baking powder, salt, and cinnamon. Make a well in the center. Pour in the egg, ½ cup of melted butter, and the milk. Stir with a wooden spoon just until the dry ingredients are moistened. Fold in the raspberries and 1 teaspoon of lemon rind. Fill each muffin cup ¾ full.

In a separate bowl combine the walnuts, ½ cup of brown sugar, ¼ cup of flour, 1 teaspoon of cinnamon, and 1 teaspoon of lemon rind. Blend in 2 tablespoons of melted butter and stir until the topping is crumbly. Sprinkle the topping over the muffins. Bake at 350° for about 20 minutes. Mix the confectioners' sugar and lemon juice, blending until smooth. Drizzle the glaze over the warm muffins.

Makes 12.

P opovers

2 eggs, at room temperature,
lightly beaten
1 cup milk, at room temperature

1 cup all-purpose flour
½ teaspoon salt

■ In a mixing bowl combine all of the ingredients. Grease 8 custard cups and warm them in the oven before filling. Once heated fill each cup ⅓ full. Bake at 425° for 35 minutes.

Makes 8.

ℬ aking Powder Biscuits

¼ cup shortening   2 teaspoons baking powder
2 cups sifted all-purpose flour   ¾ cup milk
½ teaspoon salt

■ In a bowl cut the shortening into the flour, salt, and baking powder. Add milk until the mixture resembles a soft dough. Blend lightly. Turn the dough onto a floured board and knead for about 2 minutes. Roll the dough out to ½-inch thickness. Cut the biscuits with a floured biscuit cutter. Place the biscuits on an ungreased baking sheet. Bake at 450° for 12 to 15 minutes, or until golden brown.

Makes 1 dozen.

☆ **ELVIS is honored by RCA.**

Fit For a King

# utterscotch Pinwheels

2 cups all-purpose flour
3 teaspoons baking powder
¼ teaspoon salt
⅓ cup shortening
¾ cup milk

⅓ cup butter, melted
⅓ cup packed light brown sugar
½ teaspoon cinnamon
2 tablespoons corn syrup
¼ cup chopped walnuts

■ Grease a 16-cup muffin pan. Into a mixing bowl sift the flour. Measure 2 cups and resift 3 more times with the baking powder and salt. Cut in the shortening with a pastry blender. Add the milk and blend until the dough becomes stiff. Turn the dough out onto a floured board. Knead for about 3 minutes.

Shape the dough into a rectangle about ½-inch thick. Brush with 2 tablespoons of butter. Combine 2 tablespoons of brown sugar with the cinnamon. Sprinkle the mixture over the dough. Shape the dough into a jelly roll, and cut it into 16 equal portions.

In a mixing bowl combine the remaining butter, brown sugar, syrup, and nuts. Place an equal amount into each muffin cup. Place a slice of the dough on top in each cup. Bake at 425° for about 15 to 20 minutes or until brown.

Makes 16.

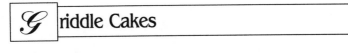# riddle Cakes

1 cup sourdough starter
2 cups warm milk
2¼ cups all-purpose flour
2 eggs

2 tablespoons sugar
2 tablespoons light corn oil
⅓ cup milk
1 teaspoon baking soda

■ In a mixing bowl whisk together all of the ingredients. Let the batter sit for about 10 minutes. Spoon 4 to 5 tablespoons of the batter onto a heated griddle. Flip when the surface bubbles, and cook until golden.

Makes 4 servings.

$\mathcal{C}$innamon Nut Bread

1 envelope active dry yeast	4 cups all-purpose flour
¼ cup warm water (115°)	½ cup walnuts, chopped
1 cup warm milk	1½ cups sugar
½ cup butter, melted	1 tablespoon cinnamon
2 eggs, well beaten	2 tablespoons grated lemon rind
½ cup sugar	¾ cup butter, melted
¼ teaspoon salt	1 egg, beaten
Juice of ½ lemon	

■ In a small bowl combine the yeast and warm water. Set the mixture aside. In a large bowl combine the milk and ½ cup of melted butter. Add the eggs, ½ cup of sugar, the salt, yeast, lemon juice, flour, and walnuts, mixing until a dough forms. Turn the dough onto a floured board and knead. Place the dough in a greased mixing bowl, cover, and let it rise until it has doubled in bulk.

Combine 1½ cups of sugar, the cinnamon, and lemon rind. Divide the dough in half and roll it out into 2 rectangles. Brush the dough rectangles with ¾ cup of melted butter, and sprinkle them with the cinnamon mixture. Beginning with a long edge, roll the dough up jelly-roll style. Press to seal the edge. Press each end and fold it under. Place the loaves on a greased baking sheet and let them rise again for 1 hour.

Brush the tops with the remaining beaten egg. Bake at 300° for 30 minutes. Cool before serving.

Makes 2 loaves.

$\mathcal{E}$LVIS'S friends were known as the "Memphis Mafia." This group of young men worked for Elvis, and in return he bought them cars, suits, homes, and jewelry. As far as Elvis was concerned, he wasn't better than them because he had money: they were his friends. He was more than generous in sharing his wealth.

☆ **PRESENTING a check to Governor Waller for the Hurricane Relief Fund in 1975**

$\mathscr{S}$ our Milk Corn Bread

2 cups sour milk
1 teaspoon baking soda
2 eggs
½ teaspoon salt

1 teaspoon sugar
¼ cup all-purpose flour, sifted
1½ cups cornmeal, sifted
¼ cup shortening, melted

■ In a mixing bowl blend the milk with the baking soda. In a separate bowl beat the eggs. Add the salt and sugar. Blend in the milk mixture, flour, and cornmeal. Stir in the melted shortening. Mix lightly but thoroughly.

Pour the batter into a hot, greased shallow baking pan. Bake at 375° for about 25 to 35 minutes or until golden.

Makes 1 loaf.

Breads

ℬasic Yeast Bread

6½ cups all-purpose flour
  2 envelopes active dry yeast
  2 cups milk
  ⅓ cup sugar

⅓ cup shortening
1½ teaspoons salt
2 eggs

■ In a large mixing bowl combine 3 cups of flour and the yeast. In a saucepan heat the milk, sugar, shortening, and salt. Stir constantly until the shortening is warm and almost melted. Add the liquid mixture to the dry mixture. Mix in the eggs. Beat with an electric mixer on low for about 3 minutes, keeping the sides of the bowl scraped. Switch to high and continue beating 3 more minutes. Add all of the remaining flour except 1 cup. The dough should become difficult to mix.

Turn the dough onto a floured board. Knead in the remaining flour until it becomes smooth and pliable. Shape the dough into a smooth ball and place it in a lightly greased bowl, turning once to grease the entire surface. Cover with a damp towel. Let the dough rise in a warm place until it has doubled in size. Punch the dough down and divide it into 2 loaves. Place them in 2 well-greased 8 x 4-inch loaf pans. Cover and let the dough rise again until nearly double in size. Bake at 375° for 35 to 40 minutes or until done. Remove the loaves from the pan and cool on a wire rack.

Makes 2 loaves.

ℭorn Bread

2 cups white cornmeal
1 cup all-purpose flour
1 tablespoon sugar
4 teaspoons baking powder

1 egg
1 teaspoon salt
Milk

■ In a mixing bowl combine all of the dry ingredients. Add the eggs and enough milk to make a smooth batter. Pour the batter into a warm, well-greased bread pan. Bake at 425° for about 25 minutes or until golden.

Makes 1 loaf.

Fit For a King

☆ **DRIVING through Memphis**

> *E*LVIS *bought a pale-green ranch home at 1034 Audubon Drive in May 1956. It was a decent place to share with his mother and father. One of his favorite activities in the new house was sitting at the kitchen table eating corn bread dunked in buttermilk.*

C orn Muffins

1½ cups sifted cornmeal	½ teaspoon baking soda
½ cup sifted all-purpose flour	1 egg
½ teaspoon salt	1 cup buttermilk
1 teaspoon baking powder	3 tablespoons shortening, melted

■ Into a mixing bowl sift together the cornmeal, flour, salt, baking powder, and baking soda. Add the eggs, buttermilk, and melted shortening. Mix thoroughly. The batter should be very thin. Pour into greased muffin cups. Bake at 425° for about 25 minutes.
   Makes 2 dozen.

Breads

_B_ anana Bread

⅓ cup butter
½ cup sugar
2 eggs
1¾ cups all-purpose flour

1 teaspoon baking powder
¼ teaspoon salt
1 cup mashed ripe bananas

■ In a mixing bowl cream the butter with the sugar. Add the eggs and beat well. In a separate bowl combine the flour, baking powder, and salt. Stir the dry ingredients into the creamed mixture. Add the bananas, blending well. Pour the batter into a greased loaf pan. Bake at 350° for about 40 minutes. Remove the bread from the pan to cool.
    Makes 1 loaf.

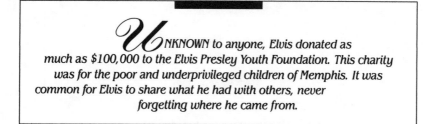

_U_ NKNOWN to anyone, Elvis donated as much as $100,000 to the Elvis Presley Youth Foundation. This charity was for the poor and underprivileged children of Memphis. It was common for Elvis to share what he had with others, never forgetting where he came from.

_B_ anana Tea Bread

1¾ cups sifted all-purpose flour
¼ teaspoon salt
2 teaspoons baking powder
¼ teaspoon baking soda

⅓ cup shortening
⅔ cup sugar
2 eggs, well beaten
1 cup mashed banana

■ In a bowl sift together the flour, salt, baking powder, and baking soda. In a separate bowl cream the shortening with the sugar. Add the eggs, beating well after each addition. Add the dry ingredients and the banana. Beat until smooth. Pour the batter into a greased loaf pan. Bake at 350° for 1 hour and 10 minutes. Let the bread cool before serving.
    Makes 1 loaf.

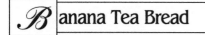

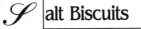 alt Biscuits

2 cups all-purpose flour
3 tablespoons baking powder
1 teaspoon salt

⅓ cup oil
1 cup milk
Coarse salt

■ In a mixing bowl combine the dry ingredients. Add the oil and ⅔ cup of milk. Fill greased muffin cups ⅔ full with batter. Flatten with the back of a spoon. Moisten the tops with the remaining milk. Sprinkle the coarse salt over each muffin. Bake at 450° for about 11 minutes.

Makes 12.

 egetable Bread

3 cups all-purpose flour
1½ cups sugar
1½ teaspoons baking soda
½ teaspoon baking powder
½ teaspoon salt
1½ teaspoons cinnamon

3 eggs
1 teaspoon vanilla extract
2 cups peeled and grated zucchini
¾ cup oil
½ cup buttermilk

■ Into a bowl sift together the flour, sugar, baking soda, baking powder, salt, and cinnamon. In a separate bowl beat together the remaining ingredients. Stir the dry ingredients into the zucchini mixture, mixing well. Pour the batter into 2 greased loaf pans. Bake at 325° for about 50 minutes or until done. Let the bread cool before serving.

Makes 2 loaves.

Breads

$\mathscr{S}$ outhern Spoon Bread

4 cups milk
1 cup cornmeal
2 teaspoons baking powder

1 teaspoon salt
2 tablespoons butter
4 eggs, well beaten

■ In a mixing bowl blend 1 cup of milk with the cornmeal. Scald 3 cups of milk in the top of a double boiler. Add the hot milk to the cornmeal mixture. Return the mixture to the top of the double boiler and cook for about 10 minutes or until the mixture is thin and smooth. Add the baking powder, salt, and butter.

Remove the batter from the double boiler and fold the beaten eggs slowly into the mixture. Pour into a buttered 1½-quart baking dish. Bake at 450° for about 45 minutes. Serve immediately.

Makes 5 servings.

☆ **TEDDY Bears became popular with Elvis fans.**

Fit For a King

$\mathcal{O}$nion Bread

2 envelopes active dry yeast	½ teaspoon salt
1 cup warm water (115°)	3 tablespoons tomato paste
2 cups all-purpose flour	1 yellow onion, peeled and chopped
Olive oil	6 green onions, chopped
1 teaspoon sugar	1 clove garlic, minced

■ In a large bowl mix the yeast with the water, and 1 cup of flour, ¼ cup of olive oil, sugar, and salt. Blend with an electric mixer until smooth. Add the remaining flour and knead by hand for 5 minutes.

Cover the dough and let it rise until doubled in bulk. Punch down and knead for about 2 minutes. Shape the dough into a loaf and place it in a greased loaf pan. Let the dough rise again. After it rises, poke holes all over it and brush with olive oil and then tomato paste.

Combine the onions and garlic, and sprinkle the mixture over the tomato paste. Bake at 375° for 30 minutes or until the top is well browned. Let the bread cool before serving.

Makes 1 loaf.

$\mathcal{S}$our Cream Blueberry Muffins

1 egg	½ teaspoon baking soda
1 cup sugar	1 teaspoon baking powder
1 cup sour cream	¼ teaspoon salt
¼ cup oil	1 cup frozen blueberries
1¾ cups all-purpose flour	

■ In a large mixing bowl beat the egg with the sugar, sour cream, and oil until thoroughly blended. In a separate bowl combine the flour, baking soda, baking powder and salt. Add the dry ingredients to the sour cream mixture. Stir in the blueberries.

Spoon the mixture into greased or paper lined muffin pans, filling each about ⅔ full. Bake at 400° for about 15 to 20 minutes or until a toothpick inserted in the center comes out clean.

Makes 1 dozen.

Breads

$\mathscr{M}$onkey Bread

2 envelopes active dry yeast	⅓ cup plus 1 tablespoon butter,
½ cup sugar	softened
¼ cup warm water (115°)	½ teaspoon salt
1 cup milk, heated	2 eggs, slightly beaten
	5½ cups all-purpose flour

Topping

1½ cups sugar	1 teaspoon cinnamon
½ cup chopped walnuts	½ cup butter, melted
2 teaspoons fresh ground ginger	

■ In a small bowl dissolve the yeast and 1 tablespoon of sugar in the water. Let the mixture stand for 5 minutes. In a large bowl combine the milk, sugar, butter, salt, and eggs. Add the yeast mixture. Beat in 3 cups of flour, beating until smooth. Add the remaining flour. Turn the dough onto a floured board and knead. Let the dough rest for 10 minutes. Knead the dough for 8 minutes more. Place the dough in a greased bowl, turning the dough greased-side up. Cover and let it rise in a warm place until doubled in bulk, about 30 minutes.

In a small bowl combine 1½ cups of sugar, the walnuts, ginger, and cinnamon. Punch the dough down and divide it into 36 portions. Roll each portion into a ball. Roll each ball first in the melted butter, then in the walnut mixture. Place the balls in a greased 10 x 4-inch loaf pan. Sprinkle any remaining topping over the dough. Cover and let the dough rise for 30 minutes. Bake at 350° for 1 hour or until golden brown. Let the bread cool before serving.

Makes 10 servings.

$\mathscr{W}$ITH all the wealth Elvis attained, money didn't mean that much to him. Sure, it allowed him the luxury to buy whatever he wanted. Yet in spite of all the expensive cars and custom homes, the Presleys remained humble.

𝒜 pple Bread

1 cup sugar	1 teaspoon baking powder
½ cup shortening	1 teaspoon baking soda
2 eggs	¼ teaspoon salt
4 medium apples	½ cup chopped walnuts
1 teaspoon vanilla extract	1 tablespoon sugar
2 cups all-purpose flour	¼ teaspoon ground cinnamon

■ Grease and flour a 9 x 5-inch loaf pan. Peel, core, and finely chop the apples. In a bowl mix 1 cup of sugar with the shortening, eggs, apples, and vanilla. Add the flour, baking powder, baking soda, and salt until smooth. Spread the batter in the prepared pan.

Mix 1 tablespoon of sugar with the cinnamon. Sprinkle the mixture over the batter. Bake at 350° for 55 minutes or until a toothpick inserted in the center comes out clean. Remove from the pan to cool.

Makes 1 loaf.

Breads

$\mathcal{C}$ ranberry Bread

2 cups all-purpose flour	¾ cup fresh orange juice
1 cup sugar	1 tablespoon grated orange rind
1½ teaspoons double acting baking powder	1 egg, well beaten
½ teaspoon baking soda	½ cup chopped walnuts
¼ teaspoon salt	2 cups coarsely chopped fresh cranberries
¼ cup shortening	

■ In a mixing bowl sift together the flour, sugar, baking powder, baking soda, and salt. Cut in the shortening until the mixture resembles coarse crumbs. Set aside. In a separate bowl combine the orange juice, orange rind, and egg. Pour the juice mixture into dry ingredients, mixing just until moist. Carefully fold in the chopped nuts and cranberries.

Spoon the batter into a greased loaf pan, spreading the corners and sides higher than in the center. Bake at 350° for 1 hour. Let the bread cool before serving.

Makes 1 loaf.

☆ TALKING with fans at the Memphis train station

Fit For a King

110

𝒞 ranberry-Apple Muffins

1 apple
1 cup whole cranberries, diced
1 cup sugar
1 egg
1 cup milk

¼ cup oil
1 cup all-purpose flour
1 tablespoon baking powder
¼ teaspoon salt

■ Peel, core, and thinly slice the apple. In a large mixing bowl toss the apples and cranberries with the sugar. Add the egg, milk, and oil. Stir just until moist. Add the flour, baking powder, and salt.

Spoon the batter into 12 greased or paper lined muffin cups, filling each about ⅔ full. Bake at 400° for 20 minutes or until a toothpick inserted in the center comes out clean. Cool before serving.

Makes 12.

ℬ anana Muffins

1½ cups all-purpose flour
1¼ teaspoons baking powder
½ teaspoon baking soda
¼ teaspoon salt
3 tablespoons sugar
2 eggs

½ pound bananas, peeled and sliced
¼ teaspoon grated lemon rind
3 tablespoons fresh lemon juice
3 tablespoons buttermilk
3 tablespoons shortening

■ Into a mixing bowl sift the flour. Measure 1½ cups and resift 3 times with the baking powder, baking soda, salt, and sugar. In a separate bowl beat the eggs. Add the sliced bananas and mash with a fork. Add the lemon rind, lemon juice, and buttermilk. Blend in the shortening. Add the liquid all at once to the dry ingredients.

Mix thoroughly and vigorously until the flour is moist. Spoon into greased muffin cups. Bake at 400° for 30 minutes or until golden. Serve hot.

Makes 1 dozen.

uttermilk Biscuits

2 cups sifted all-purpose flour	**2 tablespoons shortening**
½ teaspoon baking soda	**¾ cup buttermilk**
½ teaspoon salt	

■ In a mixing bowl combine the flour, baking soda, and salt. Cut the shortening into the dry ingredients with a pastry blender. Add the buttermilk and stir until the dough leaves the sides of the bowl. Turn the dough onto a floured board and roll to ½-inch thickness. Cut with floured biscuit cutter. Place the biscuits on a hot, greased baking sheet. Bake at 425° for about 15 minutes.

Makes 1 dozen.

eanut Butter Bread with Buttermilk

1¾ cups all-purpose flour	**⅓ cup creamy peanut butter**
1 teaspoon baking soda	**1 egg, well beaten**
¼ teaspoon salt	**1 cup thick buttermilk**
1 cup packed light brown sugar	

■ Into a mixing bowl sift the flour. Measure 1¾ cups and resift 3 times with the baking soda and salt. In a separate bowl blend together the sugar and peanut butter. Add the egg, beating well. Blend the dry ingredients into the peanut butter mixture. Add the buttermilk, beating until smooth.

Turn into a greased 8 x 4-inch loaf pan. Bake at 350° for about 1 hour or until a toothpick inserted in the center comes out clean. Remove the bread from the pan to cool.

Makes 1 loaf.

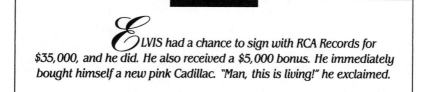

LVIS had a chance to sign with RCA Records for $35,000, and he did. He also received a $5,000 bonus. He immediately bought himself a new pink Cadillac. "Man, this is living!" he exclaimed.

☆ AT THE RCA recording studios in Nashville

ℬ acon Muffins

2 cups all-purpose flour	**2 slices of crisp bacon, crumbled**
3 teaspoons baking powder	**1 egg**
¼ teaspoon salt	**1 cup milk**
3 tablespoons sugar	**2 tablespoons bacon fat, melted**

■ Into a mixing bowl sift the flour, measure 2 cups and resift 3 times with the baking powder, salt, and sugar. Add the bacon. Beat the egg with the milk and melted fat. Add the milk mixture to the flour, stirring just until it is dampened. The batter should be somewhat blended but not too smooth. Spoon into greased muffin cups, filling each ⅔ full. Bake at 425° for 20 minutes or until brown. Serve hot.
  Makes 1 dozen.

Breads

$\mathscr{P}$otato Flour Muffins

½ cup potato flour	4 eggs, separated
1 teaspoon baking powder	2 tablespoons sugar
¼ teaspoon salt	2 tablespoons ice water

■ In a mixing bowl combine the potato flour, baking powder, and salt. Sift 3 times.

In a separate bowl beat the egg whites until they are stiff but not dry. Add the sugar and blend. Beat the egg yolks and fold them into the egg whites. Blend the dry ingredients into the egg mixture. Sprinkle a few drops of the ice water over the top and continue folding in the ingredients until all of the water is absorbed.

Spoon into well greased cast iron muffin cups. Bake at 375° for about 18 to 20 minutes. Serve hot with butter.

Makes 10.

☆ A YOUNG fan is delighted to have her picture
taken with Elvis.

Fit For a King

poon Bread with Cheese

½ cup yellow cornmeal
¼ teaspoon salt
¼ teaspoon dry mustard
Cayenne pepper to taste

1¼ cups milk
¾ cup grated American cheese
2 large eggs, separated

■ Into a mixing bowl sift the cornmeal. Resift 3 times with the salt, dry mustard, and cayenne pepper. In a saucepan blend the cold milk with the sifted ingredients. Cook over direct heat until thick and smooth, stirring constantly. Add the cheese and remove from the heat. Continue to stir until the cheese has melted. Cool slightly and add some of the hot mixture into the beaten egg yolks. Return the yolk mixture to the saucepan, heat through, and stir well. Remove the pan from heat and cool until lukewarm. In a separate bowl beat the egg whites until stiff. Fold the egg whites into the batter. Pour the batter into a well-greased glass casserole dish and bake at 375° for about 35 minutes. Serve hot with butter.

Makes 4 servings.

umpkin Bread

1 cup packed light brown sugar
½ cup sugar
1 cup canned pumpkin
½ cup oil
2 eggs, beaten
2 cups all-purpose flour
1 teaspoon baking soda

¼ teaspoon salt
½ teaspoon nutmeg
½ teaspoon cinnamon
¼ teaspoon ginger
1 cup raisins
½ cup chopped walnuts
¼ cup water

■ In a mixing bowl combine the brown sugar, sugar, pumpkin, oil, and eggs, and beat until well blended. Into a separate bowl sift together the flour, baking soda, salt, nutmeg, cinnamon, and ginger. Add the dry ingredients to the pumpkin mixture and blend well. Add the raisins, walnuts, and water. Pour the batter into a well-oiled loaf pan. Bake at 350° for 1 hour and 10 minutes or until a toothpick inserted in the center comes out clean. Let the bread cool before serving.

Makes 1 loaf.

$\mathscr{C}$offee Cake Bread

1 envelope active dry yeast	1 egg
¾ cup warm water (115°)	¼ cup butter
¼ cup sugar	¼ cup chopped walnuts
½ teaspoon salt	½ cup raisins
2¼ cups sifted all-purpose flour	

■ In a mixing bowl dissolve the yeast in the warm water. Add the sugar, salt, and half the flour. Beat for 2 minutes. Beat in the egg and butter. Add the remaining flour and blend. Add the nuts and raisins.

Place the dough in a greased loaf pan. Let the dough rise until doubled in bulk. Bake at 375° for 35 minutes or until brown. Remove the loaf from the pan. Serve warm.

Makes 1 loaf.

$\mathscr{P}$ineapple Coffee Cake

1½ cups sifted all-purpose flour	2 eggs
1 cup sugar	1 cup sour cream
2 teaspoons baking powder	½ teaspoon vanilla extract
½ teaspoon baking soda	¼ cup pineapple chunks, drained
¼ teaspoon salt	

Topping

5 tablespoons sugar	½ teaspoon cinnamon
2 tablespoons butter	

■ In a large bowl sift together the flour, 1 cup of sugar, baking powder, baking soda, and salt. In a separate bowl beat together the eggs, sour cream, and vanilla. Add the sour cream mixture to the dry ingredients and beat until smooth. Pour the batter into a 9-inch square baking pan. Dot with pineapple chunks. Blend all of the ingredients for the topping until crumbly. Sprinkle over the batter. Bake at 350° for 20 to 25 minutes.

Makes 9 squares.

Fit For a King

Orange Nut Bread

¼ cup butter
1 cup packed light brown sugar
2 eggs
1 tablespoon grated orange rind
3 cups all-purpose flour
3 teaspoons baking powder

½ teaspoon baking soda
¼ teaspoon salt
½ cup fresh orange juice
½ cup milk
½ cup chopped walnuts

■ In a mixing bowl cream the butter with the brown sugar. Add the eggs one at a time, beating well after each addition. Stir in the orange rind and creamed butter. Into a separate bowl sift the flour. Measure 3 cups and sift again with the baking powder, baking soda, and salt. Add the dry ingredients to the batter alternately with the orange juice and milk, mixing well. Fold in the nuts. Pour the batter into 2 small greased loaf pans. Bake at 350° for about 1 hour and 20 minutes. Let the bread cool before serving.
    Makes 2 small loaves.

Dill Bread

1 envelope active dry yeast
¼ cup warm water (115°)
1 cup cream-style cottage cheese
1 tablespoon butter
2 tablespoons sugar
½ teaspoon salt

¼ teaspoon baking soda
1 teaspoon minced onion
1 teaspoon dillweed
1 teaspoon dill seed
1 egg
2¼ cups all-purpose flour

■ In a small bowl combine the yeast and water. Let the mixture stand for about 10 minutes. In a saucepan heat the cottage cheese until lukewarm. In a mixing bowl combine the cottage cheese, butter, sugar, salt, and baking soda. Add the onion, dillweed, dill seed, egg, and yeast. Beat until well blended. Add the flour, mixing until a dough forms. Cover and let the dough rise until doubled in bulk. Beat the dough down and place it in a greased loaf pan. Let the dough rise for about 30 minutes. Bake at 350° for 35 to 40 minutes or until the crust is golden brown.
    Makes 1 loaf.

Blueberry Muffins

2 cups all-purpose flour	⅔ cup sugar
3 teaspoons baking powder	1 egg
½ teaspoon salt	¾ cup milk
⅓ cup butter	1 cup blueberries

■ Into a mixing bowl sift the flour with the baking powder and salt. In a separate bowl cream together the butter and sugar. Add the egg and milk, and beat until fluffy.

Add the flour mixture to the creamed butter a little at a time. Add the blueberries. Spoon the batter into greased muffin cups, filling each ¾ full. Bake at 425° for 18 minutes or until brown.

Makes 12.

Zucchini Muffins

3 cups all-purpose flour	2 cups sugar
1 teaspoon baking powder	4 eggs
1 teaspoon baking soda	1 cup oil
½ teaspoon salt	2 cups peeled and grated zucchini
1 teaspoon cinnamon	½ teaspoon vanilla extract

■ Into a bowl sift the flour, baking powder, baking soda, salt, and cinnamon. In a separate bowl combine the sugar and eggs, beating well. Gradually add the oil and continue to beat for 3 to 5 minutes. Add the zucchini and vanilla. Add the dry ingredients to the zucchini mixture, blending until the batter is smooth. Spoon the batter into greased muffin cups, filling each ⅔ full. Bake at 350° for 25 minutes or until golden brown.

Makes 12 muffins.

☆ **EATING one of his favorite foods: a cheeseburger**

*O*N OCTOBER 24, 1956, Variety, in a front-page banner-headline story titled, "Elvis a Millionaire in One Year," reported that his gross income was derived from record royalties ($450,000) movie deals ($250,000), TV appearances ($100,000), and personal appearances ($200,000). It was expected that Elvis merchandise would sell over $40 million in the next fifteen months. Other deals in the works included 18,000 ice cream locations and 30,000 hamburger stands selling "Hounddogs" (large hot dogs) and "Presley Burgers."

atmeal Bread

1¾ cups oats
1 cup buttermilk
1¾ cups all-purpose flour

1 teaspoon salt
1 teaspoon cream of tartar
1 teaspoon baking soda

■ In a mixing bowl soak the oats in the buttermilk. In a separate bowl combine the remaining ingredients. Add the dry ingredients to the oatmeal mixture, mixing until a dough forms. Turn the dough onto a floured surface and knead lightly. Place the dough in a greased loaf pan. Bake at 400° for about 35 minutes.

Makes 1 loaf.

$\mathcal{M}$AIN $\mathcal{D}$ISHES

$\mathcal{C}$ heeseburgers

1½ pounds ground beef
¼ cup cold milk
1 teaspoon salt
Pepper to taste
⅓ cup chili sauce
3 tablespoons pickle relish

2 teaspoons mustard
⅓ cup butter
6 hamburger buns, buttered and
  toasted
6 slices American cheese

■ In a large mixing bowl combine the ground beef, milk, salt, and pepper. Form into 6 patties. Slice the cheese to fit the hamburger buns. In a small bowl blend together the chili sauce, relish, and mustard.

In a skillet melt the butter. Pan-fry the patties for about 12 minutes, turning several times as they cook. Place on hamburger buns. Spread each with the relish mixture. Top with cheese. Place the patties under the broiler, cooking until the cheese begins to melt.

Makes 6 servings.

 *S A BOY who grew up poor and lived
in the projects, Elvis learned the value of money at an early age.
"My parents couldn't afford to buy me the toys I wanted for Christmas.
I found out that one year our Christmas basket filled
with goodies was given to us by charity."*

# Pork Chops with Sauerkraut

8 pork chops	2 tablespoons Dijon mustard
2 tablespoons butter	½ cup applesauce
Salt and pepper to taste	1 tablespoon cornstarch
2 16-ounce cans sauerkraut	2 tablespoons cold water

■ In a large skillet sauté the pork chops in the butter until lightly browned on both sides. Season with salt and pepper. Rinse the sauerkraut under cold running water. Drain the excess liquid.

Place the sauerkraut in a baking dish. Add the mustard and applesauce. Arrange the pork chops over the sauerkraut mixture. Cover and bake at 350° for 50 minutes. Dissolve the cornstarch in the water. Blend the cornstarch into the sauerkraut mixture to thicken.

Makes 8 servings.

☆ CONSTANTLY surrounded by fans, Elvis doesn't seem
to mind the attention.

Fit For a King

ork Chops with Cranberries

6 pork chops
Salt to taste
4 cups ground cranberries

¾ cup honey
½ teaspoon cloves

■ In a skillet brown the pork chops. Season with salt. In a bowl combine the cranberries, honey, and cloves. Place 3 of the chops in a greased baking dish. Spread half the cranberries over the pork chops. Arrange the remaining pork chops on top. Cover with the remaining cranberries. Cover and bake at 350° for 1 hour.
Makes 6 servings.

arbecued Baby Back Pork Ribs

2 tablespoons bacon drippings
1 medium onion, finely chopped
1 clove garlic, minced
1 14-ounce bottle ketchup
6 tablespoons Worcestershire sauce
2 tablespoons cider vinegar
¼ cup dry white wine
1 teaspoon dry mustard
2 tablespoons packed dark brown sugar

1½ tablespoons ground hot red chiles
1½ tablespoons ground mild red chiles
¼ teaspoon cayenne pepper
½ teaspoon cumin
¼ teaspoon coriander
1 teaspoon liquid smoke
6 pounds baby back pork ribs, in uncut racks

■ In a saucepan melt the bacon drippings over medium heat. Add the onion and garlic. Sauté until the onion is transparent. Add the remaining ingredients except the ribs. Reduce the heat and simmer uncovered for about 15 minutes, stirring occasionally.

Prepare the grill. Position the rack 3 inches above the heat source, and sear the meat 2 minutes per side. Raise the rack 2 inches and cover it with aluminum foil. Puncture to create ventilation. Place the ribs on the foil and brush with the sauce. Cook for about 15 minutes. Turn and brush with sauce. Grill for 10 minutes. Turn and baste again. The ribs should have a crisp glaze. Transfer to a carving board. Cut the ribs apart and place them on a serving platter.
Makes 8 to 12 servings.

Main Dishes

arbecued Pork Chops with Coriander

2 cloves garlic, crushed
1 tablespoon coriander
8 black peppercorns, crushed
1 teaspoon packed light brown
   sugar

3 tablespoons soy sauce
4 pork loin chops, each 1-inch thick

■ In a mixing bowl combine the garlic, coriander, peppercorns, brown sugar, and soy sauce. Brush the chops with the mixture. Cover and marinate for 30 minutes. Grill the chops for 10 to 12 minutes per side over moderate coals. Brush with sauce.
   Makes 4 servings.

alt Pork in Cream Gravy

1 tablespoon bacon fat
¾ pound salt pork, cut into ⅛-inch
   thick strips

All-purpose flour
2 cups milk
1 teaspoon chopped parsley

■ In a skillet melt the bacon fat. Dip strips of the pork into the flour, and fry in the hot bacon fat until brown and crisp. Remove the salt pork strips and drain all but ¼ cup of the fat. To that add 4 tablespoons of flour, blending until smooth. Gradually add the milk, stirring constantly until thick and smooth. Simmer for about 5 minutes. If the gravy is too thick, add more milk. Serve with crisp salt pork. Sprinkle with parsley.
   Makes 4 servings.

> *$\mathcal{A}$ GIRL dating Elvis usually found herself driving around for hours with him in his car, then stopping when possible at some nondescript hamburger stand for a sandwich and a coke.*

☆ **A CLASSIC Elvis pose**

$\mathscr{S}$ moked Oven Pork

3 tablespoons soy sauce
2 tablespoons hoisin sauce
2 tablespoons honey

½ teaspoon garlic salt
3 pounds pork loin

■ In a shallow saucepan combine the soy sauce, hoisin sauce, honey, and garlic. Add the pork and rub the mixture over the entire surface. Marinate the pork for 8 hours at room temperature, turning occasionally.

Preheat the oven to 425°. Roast the pork loin for 20 minutes. Transfer the loin to a smoke oven, and smoke for about 40 minutes or until a meat thermometer inserted in the thickest part of the meat registers 160°. Slice and serve.

Makes 6 servings.

Main Dishes

an Broiled Pork Chops & Potatoes

4 loin pork chops, each 1-inch thick	1 tablespoon all-purpose flour
1½ teaspoons salt	½ cup milk
2 potatoes, peeled	½ cup water
2 tablespoons water	

■ Heat a skillet and sprinkle the bottom with flour. Add the pork chops. Lift and place again in the flour to prevent sticking. Cook quickly until chops are brown on both sides. Sprinkle with salt. Cover the skillet and reduce the heat. Simmer for 10 minutes.

Slice the potatoes lengthwise into thirds. Arrange the potato slices flat around the pork chops. Sprinkle with the remaining salt. Cover and cook for 30 minutes. Turn the pork chops and potatoes once more. Add ¼ cup of water. When both are tender and brown remove the chops and potatoes to a platter. Drain all but 1 tablespoon of fat from the skillet. Return the skillet to the heat.

Add the flour to the fat, blending until smooth. Add the milk and ¼ cup of water, and bring the gravy to a boil. As it cooks, stir constantly, scraping the skillet. Cook until smooth and thick. Serve with the pork chops.

Makes 4 servings.

ork Chops with Sweet Peppers

2 tablespoons oil	1 bay leaf
1¾ pounds pork chops	¼ teaspoon paprika
Salt and pepper to taste	¼ teaspoon thyme
½ cup diced onion	2 red bell peppers, cut into strips
¼ teaspoon garlic salt	2 tablespoons sour cream
¼ cup dry white wine	2 tablespoons heavy cream
½ cup beef broth	

■ In a saucepan heat the oil. Season the pork chops with the salt and pepper to taste. Brown the chops in the heated oil. Remove the excess fat. Add the onions and garlic, and sauté for 3 minutes. Add the wine, broth, bay leaf, paprika, and thyme, and bring the wine to a boil. Cover and cook for about 15 minutes. Remove the cover and place the red pepper strips over the meat. Cook for 5 minutes. Remove the pork chops. Add the sour cream and heavy cream, stirring to blend. Remove the bay leaf before serving. Pour the sauce over the pork chops before serving.

Makes 4 servings.

Fit For a King

# ork Chops with Vegetables

2 tablespoons oil
6 pork loin chops, cut ½-inch thick
1 green bell pepper, cut into strips
2 tablespoons all-purpose flour
1 10-ounce can condensed onion
  soup

2 tablespoons Worcestershire sauce
1 teaspoon garlic powder
1 teaspoon salt
2 medium tomatoes, cut into wedges

■ In a large skillet heat the oil. Brown the pork chops three at a time on both sides and remove them from the skillet. Sauté the green peppers for 1 minute and remove them. Add the flour to the skillet, blending well, and cook for 1 minute. Blend in the onion soup, Worcestershire sauce, garlic powder, and salt. Bring the mixture to a boil. Return the chops to the skillet, basting them with sauce. Cover and simmer until the chops are tender, about 1 hour. Blend in the tomatoes and green peppers. Cover and simmer 5 minutes more.

Makes 6 servings.

# am & Cheese Casserole

2 teaspoons butter
8 slices white bread
1⅓ cups ground cooked ham
½ teaspoon dry mustard
1 tablespoon milk
1½ teaspoons prepared mustard

1½ cups grated American cheese
1½ cups milk
3 eggs
Salt and pepper to taste
1 teaspoon finely chopped parsley

■ Grease an 8-inch baking dish. Trim the crusts from the bread. Layer the bottom of the baking dish with 4 slices of bread. In a large mixing bowl combine the ham, dry mustard, and 1 tablespoon of milk. Spread the ham mixture evenly on the bread slices in the dish. Spread the prepared mustard over the ham. Sprinkle the cheese over all. Cut the remaining 4 slices of bread in half diagonally, and place them over the cheese. Cut through all of the layers with a sharp knife.

In a mixing bowl combine 1½ cups of milk with the eggs and seasonings, beating well. Pour the mixture evenly over the bread. Let the casserole stand for about 10 minutes to allow the bread to absorb the liquid. Bake at 325° for 55 minutes. Garnish with parsley.

Makes 6 servings.

Main Dishes

am & Sweet Potato Casserole

1½ cups cooked ham, diced
1 tablespoon butter
1½ pounds hot sweet potatoes,
   mashed
2 eggs, beaten

½ cup milk
1½ tablespoons fresh lemon juice
Salt to taste

■ In a skillet lightly brown the ham in the butter. In a bowl whip the potatoes until smooth. Add the eggs, milk, lemon juice, and salt. Fold in the diced ham. Pour the mixture into a greased casserole dish. Bake at 350° for about 45 minutes.

Makes 6 servings.

ountry Baked Ham

1 1-inch thick ham steak
Pepper and thyme to taste
1½ cups canned tomatoes

1 cup grated American cheese
¼ cup minced onion
Fresh parsley, chopped

■ Place the ham in a greased casserole dish with a tight fitting cover. Season with pepper and thyme. In a mixing bowl blend the tomatoes, cheese, onion, and parsley. Pour the mixture over the ham. Cover and bake at 350° for about 45 minutes. Turn once during the baking process.

Makes 4 servings.

eef & Kidney Bean Casserole

1 tablespoon butter
1 pound ground beef
1 teaspoon salt

2½ cups canned tomatoes
2½ cups drained kidney beans
½ cup buttered bread crumbs

■ Grease an 8-cup casserole dish. In a skillet melt the butter. Brown the meat. Add the salt and tomatoes. In the prepared dish alternate layers of meat mixture with the kidney beans. Top with the bread crumbs. Bake at 350° for 40 minutes.

Makes 6 servings.

Fit For a King

☆ OUTSIDE the RCA studio in Los Angeles

*M*eatball Sandwiches

1½ pounds ground beef	Bread crumbs
2 tablespoons water	3 tablespoons shortening
1½ teaspoons salt	3 medium tomatoes
Pepper to taste	1 medium onion, sliced
1 egg, beaten	5 hamburger buns
1 tablespoon milk	

■ In a bowl blend the beef with the water, salt, and pepper. Form into small balls. In a separate mixing bowl beat the egg and milk together. Dip the meatballs into the egg mixture, and then roll them in the bread crumbs.

In a heavy skillet melt the shortening. Brown the meatballs on all sides. Place the tomatoes into a food processor and blend. The tomatoes should be somewhat chunky. Pour the tomato mixture into the buns. Add the onions and meatballs.

Makes 5 servings.

Main Dishes

129

☆ **GETTING ready for a press conference in Hollywood**

ℋamburger Turnovers

1 pound ground beef	**1 tablespoon grated onion**
Salt and pepper to taste	**1 teaspoon Worcestershire sauce**
Nutmeg to taste	**3 tablespoons tomato purée**
1 tablespoon parsley, chopped	**Pastry dough**

■ In a bowl combine all of the ingredients except the pastry. Roll out the pastry dough thin. Cut into rectangles measuring 2 x 4 inches. Place a spoonful of the meat in the lower half of the dough. Moisten the edges with water and fold the pastry over the meat. Pinch the edges closed. Prick twice. Place the turnovers on a greased baking sheet. Bake at 400° for 20 to 25 minutes.

Makes 6 servings.

Fit For a King

ℋamburger & Corn Pie

¾ pound ground beef
2 tablespoons chopped onion
½ teaspoon salt
Pepper to taste
¼ teaspoon paprika
2½ tablespoons all-purpose flour

¾ cup water
4 tablespoons butter
2 cups corn
Salt and pepper to taste
1 green bell pepper, sliced

■ In a skillet brown the beef with the onions. Add the salt, pepper, and paprika. In a bowl blend the flour with the water. Add the mixture to the beef. Cook about 2 minutes, stirring constantly.

In a saucepan melt the butter. Add the corn, salt, and pepper, and cook for 3 minutes.

Grease a 10-inch glass pie pan. Pour in half of the corn. Bake at 425° for about 15 minutes. Remove and add the hamburger and rest of the corn. Garnish with green peppers. Return the pie to the oven. Bake for 15 minutes or until the bottom and top are brown.

Makes 4 servings.

ℋamburger in Sour Cream

1½ pounds ground beef
1 onion, chopped
½ teaspoon salt
Pepper to taste
3 tablespoons oil

Fresh parsley
¾ teaspoon prepared mustard
½ teaspoon soy sauce
¾ cup sour cream

■ Season the meat with the onion, salt, and pepper. Mix thoroughly. Shape into 6 patties. In a skillet heat the oil and brown the patties on both sides. Place the cooked patties in a warm oven.

In the skillet blend the pan juices with the parsley, remaining seasonings, and sour cream. Bring the mixture to a boil. Reduce the heat and simmer for 5 minutes, stirring constantly. Pour the sauce over the burgers.

Makes 6 servings.

 an Broiled Hamburgers

1¼ pound ground beef
2 tablespoons minced onion
Salt and pepper to taste

¼ cup hot water
1 tablespoon all-purpose flour

■ In a large bowl combine the hamburger, onion, salt, and pepper. Measure out the meat in ⅓ cup portions and shape into patties about ½-inch thick.

Sprinkle ¼ teaspoon of salt in the bottom of a heavy skillet. Brown both sides of the patties. Cover and reduce the heat. Cook to the desired doneness. Remove the hamburgers and add the hot water to the skillet. Blend in the flour. Increase the heat and scrape the skillet to make pan gravy. Pour the gravy over the patties.

Makes 4 servings.

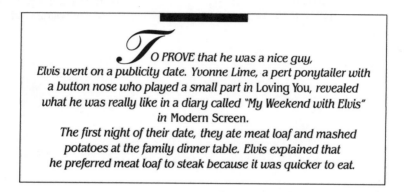

*T*O PROVE *that he was a nice guy,*
Elvis went on a publicity date. Yvonne Lime, a pert ponytailer with
a button nose who played a small part in Loving You, *revealed*
what he was really like in a diary called "My Weekend with Elvis"
in Modern Screen.
The first night of their date, they ate meat loaf and mashed
potatoes at the family dinner table. Elvis explained that
he preferred meat loaf to steak because it was quicker to eat.

eat Loaf

1½ pounds ground beef
1 egg, beaten
1 cup milk
1¼ teaspoons salt

Pepper to taste
1 cup bread crumbs
Gravy or tomato sauce

■ In a large mixing bowl combine the beef and egg. Add the milk, mixing thoroughly. Add the salt, pepper, and bread crumbs. Shape into a loaf. Place the loaf in a lightly oiled glass pan. Bake at 350° for 1 hour or until the meat is brown and the inside is cooked. Serve with gravy or tomato sauce.

Makes 6 servings.

Fit For a King

☆ **ELVIS with Yvonne Lime**

C reole Lamb Shoulder Chops

2½ pounds lamb shoulder chops
1½ teaspoons butter
   2 teaspoons salt

⅓ cup sliced onions
1½ cups tomato juice
2 medium carrots, sliced

■ Wipe the lamb chops clean. In a skillet melt the butter. Brown the lamb slowly on both sides. Add the remaining ingredients and cover tightly. Simmer for 1 hour and 30 minutes or until tender.

   Makes 6 servings.

Main Dishes

133

$\mathscr{S}$ crambled Eggs

4 eggs
2 tablespoons cream
Salt and pepper to taste

2 slices cooked bacon, crumbled
1½ teaspoons butter
¼ cup diced onion

■ In a mixing bowl beat the eggs with the cream. Season to taste with salt and pepper. Add the bacon. In a skillet melt the butter, tilting the skillet to coat the bottom. Sauté the onions. Reduce the heat to low. Add the egg mixture, stirring frequently until set. Turn the eggs onto a hot platter to serve.

Makes 2 servings.

$\mathscr{A}$T DAWN, the partiers topped their merriment with scrambled eggs cooked just the way Elvis liked them: hard as rocks.

$\mathscr{C}$ reole Eggs

2 tablespoons butter
2 tablespoons all-purpose flour
1 cup tomato juice
¼ cup diced celery
2 tablespoons minced green bell
  pepper

1 teaspoon chopped onion
Allspice to taste
Salt and pepper to taste
6 hard-boiled eggs
2 tablespoons chopped parsley
Toast or biscuits

■ In a saucepan melt the butter. Blend in the flour until smooth. Gradually add the tomato juice, stirring constantly. Add the celery, green pepper, onion, allspice, salt, and pepper.

Cook, stirring constantly, until the mixture boils and thickens. Peel the eggs and remove the yolks. Chop the egg whites and add them to the mixture. Serve with toast or biscuits. Garnish with chopped egg yolks.

Makes 4 servings.

$\mathscr{S}$ panish Omelet

Butter
 1 small onion, chopped
 ¼ cup diced green bell pepper
 ¼ cup diced red bell pepper
 1 6-ounce can tomato paste
 ¼ tablespoon Worcestershire sauce

Salt and pepper to taste
 ¼ pound mushrooms, chopped
 1 tablespoon butter
 3 large eggs
 3 tablespoons milk

■ In a skillet melt enough butter to coat the bottom. Sauté the onion until tender. Add the peppers and tomato paste. Cook until the peppers are tender. Add the Worcestershire sauce and season with salt and pepper. In a separate skillet melt a small amount of butter and sauté the mushrooms. Fold the sautéed mushrooms into the tomato mixture. In a small bowl beat the eggs with the milk. In the skillet used for the mushrooms melt 1 tablespoon of butter. Pour the eggs into the skillet and cook over medium-low heat until partially set. Pour some of the tomato mixture over half of the eggs. Fold over half of the omelet, enclosing the sauce. Let the top set. Flip the omelet onto a plate and pour the remaining sauce over the top.

Makes 1 serving.

$\mathscr{S}$ picy Lime Chicken

2 tablespoons fresh lime juice
 3 tablespoons olive oil
 2 cloves garlic, crushed
 ¼ teaspoon red pepper flakes
 Salt to taste

4 boneless chicken breasts
 1 small avocado, peeled and cubed
 1 medium tomato, sliced
 1 red onion, sliced

■ In a small bowl whisk together the lime juice, olive oil, garlic, and red pepper. Add salt to taste. Pour the sauce over the chicken and set it aside to marinate for 15 minutes. Place the chicken in a broiler pan. Reserve the marinade. Broil the chicken until done.

In a separate bowl combine the avocado, tomato, onion, and lime marinade. Spoon the mixture over the chicken just before serving.

Makes 4 servings.

$\mathcal{M}$int-glazed Barbecue Lamb

½ cup mint jelly
½ cup apple cider vinegar
1 tablespoon butter
1 teaspoon grated lemon rind
1 teaspoon fresh lemon juice
½ teaspoon dry mustard

¼ teaspoon salt
2 tablespoons rosemary
1 6-pound leg of lamb, trimmed,
  boned, and butterflied
2 cloves garlic, quartered
1 teaspoon salt

■ In a saucepan combine the mint jelly, vinegar, butter, lemon rind, lemon juice, dry mustard, and ¼ teaspoon of salt. Stir over low heat until the jelly and butter have melted. Increase the heat and bring the mixture just to boiling. Remove the glaze from the heat and add the rosemary. Stir well and let the glaze cool.

Score the skin side of the lamb at 1-inch intervals. Make 8 tiny slits at various intervals and insert a piece of garlic in each. Sprinkle the surface with salt. Place the lamb in a large, shallow baking pan. Pour the glaze over the lamb, and allow it to marinate for 3 hours at room temperature. Turn the lamb occasionally.

Heat the grill. Remove the lamb from the pan, reserving the glaze. Barbecue the lamb on the grill for about 12 minutes per side, or until well browned. Serve with the remaining glaze.

Makes 6 to 8 servings.

$\mathcal{T}$HERE is no doubt that Elvis Presley shared his wealth freely with others. There didn't have to be any reason for it. His generosity became as well known as his curling lips and swiveling hips.
To a blind man selling pencils on the street, he gave $500. To the Jerry Lewis Muscular Dystrophy Telethon, he gave $5,000. Elvis would have given the shirt off his back to anyone who knew him.
Every year during the Christmas holidays, he gave $100,000 to local charities. And to Mary Jenkins, he gave new one-hundred-dollar bills, just because he liked her macaroni salad.

$\mathscr{C}$ arolina Barbecue Chicken

1 cup ketchup	½ cup unsalted butter
1 cup apple cider vinegar	1½ teaspoons salt
1 cup water	1 teaspoon cayenne pepper
4 tablespoons packed light brown	¼ cup Worcestershire sauce
sugar	8 pounds chicken, cut into serving
½ cup mustard	pieces

■ In a saucepan combine all of the ingredients except the chicken. Cook for 30 minutes or until thickened slightly. Set aside.

Prepare the barbecue grill. Position the rack 5 inches above the heat source. Sear the chicken, skin side down, for 2 minutes.

Remove the chicken. Cover the rack with heavy-duty aluminum foil. Puncture to create ventilation. Place the chicken on the foil, skin side down.

Generously brush the chicken with the barbecue sauce. Grill until the sauce is set. Continue basting and turning until the pieces are done, about 50 minutes. To test for doneness, insert the tip of a sharp knife into the largest piece of chicken. If the juice runs clear, it is done.

Makes 12 to 15 servings.

$\mathscr{C}$ hicken Breasts with Cheese

3 whole boneless chicken breasts,	6 slices boiled ham
split in half and pounded thin	2 tomatoes, sliced
Salt and pepper to taste	1½ cups shredded Mozzarella cheese
½ cup all-purpose flour	¼ cup grated Parmesan cheese
2 tablespoons oil	¼ cup chicken broth
2 tablespoons butter	

■ Season the chicken with salt and pepper. Roll each piece in the flour and shake off the excess.

In a large skillet heat the oil and butter over medium-high heat. When the butter stops foaming add the chicken. Cook about 4 minutes on each side, until evenly browned.

Place the chicken in a baking dish. Cover each breast with a slice of ham. Top each with a slice of tomato. Sprinkle evenly with Mozzarella and Parmesan. Pour the broth over the chicken. Bake at 375° for about 10 minutes or until the cheese is bubbling.

Makes 4 servings.

Main Dishes

137

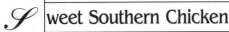

$\mathcal{S}$ weet Southern Chicken

1 cup ketchup	1 small lemon, thinly sliced
2 tablespoons honey	Red pepper sauce to taste
3 tablespoons fresh lemon juice	Salt and freshly ground pepper to
1 tablespoon Worcestershire sauce	taste
4 large cloves garlic, finely minced	1 3-pound chicken, cut into serving
4 tablespoons oil	pieces

■ In a saucepan combine all of the ingredients except the chicken. Bring the mixture to a boil over medium-high heat, stirring occasionally. Reduce the heat to low and simmer for 20 minutes. Place the chicken in a shallow dish and pour the ketchup mixture over all. Marinate the chicken in the sauce for 2 hours at room temperature.

Prepare the barbecue grill. Cover the rack with a layer of heavy-duty aluminum foil. Puncture to create ventilation. Position the rack 5 inches above the heat source. Remove the chicken from the sauce. Place the chicken on the foil skin-side up and cover the grill with a lid. Cook the chicken slowly. Baste the chicken frequently with the sauce. Turn the pieces after 30 minutes.

Continue cooking and basting the chicken for 30 to 40 minutes more or until tender and smoky. When the chicken is done, remove it from the grill and serve it with the remaining sauce.

Makes 6 servings.

$\mathcal{T}$HE WEDDING of Elvis and Priscilla was followed by a reception and champagne breakfast at the Las Vegas Aladdin Hotel. Among the dishes served were suckling pig and southern-fried chicken, as well as such elegant fare as Oysters Rockefeller. The bride and groom cut a six-tiered wedding cake decorated with red and pink hearts that were studded with tiny pearls. The band played many of Elvis's hits, including "Love Me Tender."

☆ **PRISCILLA and Elvis in Palm Springs after their wedding in Las Vegas**

$\mathcal{G}$ rilled Lemon Chicken

⅓ cup butter
¼ cup fresh lemon juice
3 tablespoons water
1 tablespoon soy sauce
½ teaspoon paprika
1 teaspoon honey

½ teaspoon Dijon mustard
1 clove garlic, minced
Salt to taste
Cayenne pepper to taste
1 whole chicken, quartered

■ In a small saucepan combine the butter, lemon juice, water, soy sauce, paprika, honey, mustard, garlic, salt, and cayenne pepper. Heat until the butter melts, stirring well. Place the chicken in a shallow dish and pour the lemon mixture over all. Marinate the chicken for about 1 hour. Grill the chicken over medium-hot coals for about 15 minutes per side. Brush frequently with sauce.

Makes 4 servings.

Main Dishes

$\mathscr{A}$ labama Barbecued Chicken

4 cups tomato sauce	1 tablespoon ground hot red chiles
½ cup light soy sauce	1 tablespoon freshly ground black
½ cup white vinegar	pepper
1 12-ounce can beer	3 large cloves garlic, finely minced
¾ tablespoon salt	8 3-pound chickens, quartered

■ In a saucepan combine all of the ingredients except the chicken. Allow the sauce to simmer over low heat for about 20 minutes. Stir frequenty.

Place the chicken pieces in large oiled baking pans, skin-side up. Bake at 450° for 45 minutes. Remove the chicken from the oven. Drain the collected pan juices and fat, measuring 1 cup. Add the pan juices to the sauce. Bring the sauce to a boil. Reduce the heat and simmer about 15 minutes. Pour the sauce over the chicken and marinate it at room temperature for about 1 hour.

Prepare the barbecue grill. Cover the rack with a layer of heavy-duty aluminum foil. Puncture to create ventilation. Position the rack 5 inches above the heat source. Remove the chicken from the sauce. Place on the foil, skin-side up. Cover the grill. Cook the chicken slowly, basting frequently with the sauce.

Turn the pieces after 30 minutes. Continue cooking and basting the chicken for 30 to 40 minutes more or until tender. Serve with the remaining sauce.

Makes 12 to 15 servings.

$\mathscr{D}$ ixie Chicken

½ cup sugar	1 egg
½ cup soy sauce	Oil
1 teaspoon ginger	4 boneless chicken breasts, cut
1 teaspoon garlic salt	into 1-inch cubes

■ In a bowl combine all of the ingredients except the oil and chicken. Blend thoroughly. Add the chicken and marinate for 1 hour. Coat each piece lightly in flour.

In a large skillet heat enough oil to fry the chicken. Fry until golden brown.

Makes 4 servings.

Fit For a King

140

$\mathcal{T}$ exas-style Barbecued Chicken

½ cup apple cider vinegar
2 tablespoons packed light brown sugar
1 tablespoon mustard
1 teaspoon salt
½ teaspoon fresh ground pepper
2 tablespoons fresh lemon juice
1 cup finely diced onion
½ cup unsalted butter, cut into 6 pieces

1 15-ounce can tomato sauce
2 tablespoons Worcestershire sauce
¼ teaspoon dried sage
¼ teaspoon basil
¼ teaspoon rosemary
¼ teaspoon thyme
1 6-pound chicken, cut into serving pieces

■ In a saucepan combine the vinegar, brown sugar, mustard, salt, pepper, lemon juice, onion, and butter. Bring the mixture to a boil over high heat. Reduce the heat and simmer for 20 minutes, stirring occasionally. Add the tomato sauce and Worcestershire sauce. Simmer for 15 minutes, stirring occasionally. Add the seasonings and reduce the heat to low. Cook the sauce for about 5 minutes. Remove it from the heat and let it cool. Refrigerate the sauce until chilled.

Prepare the barbecue grill. Position the rack 5 inches above the heat source. Place the chicken pieces skin-side down. Sear, turn, and grill until light golden brown. Remove the chicken.

Cover the rack with a layer of heavy-duty aluminum foil. Puncture to create ventilation. Place the chicken on the foil skin-side down. Spoon on the barbecue sauce. Grill until the sauce is set. Repeat until all of the pieces are brown, about 50 minutes.

Makes 8 servings.

$\mathcal{E}$ LVIS'S favorite restaurants were: Chenault's, 1402 Elvis Presley Boulevard, Memphis. Elvis and the guys used to hang out in the Delta Room in back. The specialty of the house is biscuits and sorghum syrup. The Gridiron, 4101 Elvis Presley Boulevard, Memphis. Open all night, it was a favorite source of well-done hamburgers.

☆ **ENJOYING a game of touch football**

*W*HILE *visiting her son in Hollywood,*
Gladys prepared for Elvis all of his favorites: sauerkraut and bacon,
mashed potatoes with gravy, and peas cooked with pork.
At the studio commissary he would forego the menu for bacon burnt
to a crisp, and peanut butter and mashed banana sandwiches—all
washed down with four glasses of milk. Over and over again, Elvis
would say, "The only food I truly like is my mother's hominy grits,
country ham, corn pone, biscuits, fried corn, and okra."
If he needed to shed some weight for a particular picture, Elvis
skipped lunch altogether and played touch football.

Fit For a King

erfect Fried Chicken

¾ cup all-purpose flour
1½ teaspoons salt
1½ teaspoons paprika

¼ teaspoon pepper
1 3-pound broiler fryer, cut up
Oil

■ In a paper bag combine the flour and seasonings. Add a few chicken pieces at a time, and shake. Remove the chicken to a plate and let the coating dry. In a skillet heat ½ inch of oil. Lightly brown the meaty sides of the chicken first. Lightly brown the other side. Reduce the heat and cover. Simmer for 30 minutes. Uncover for the last 10 minutes.

Makes 4 servings.

hicken Pie

1 broiler-fryer chicken
2 cups water
1½ teaspoons salt
¼ teaspoon pepper
2 cups diced celery

½ cup light cream
¼ cup all-purpose flour
1 pimiento, chopped
Pastry for a 2-crust pie

■ In a saucepan with a tight fitting lid combine the chicken, water, salt, pepper, and celery. Bring the water to a boil. Reduce the heat, cover, and simmer for 40 minutes. The chicken should be tender. Remove the chicken from the stock. Strain the stock and return it to the saucepan. Boil until the stock is reduced by 2 cups. Remove it from the heat.

Remove the skin and bones. Dice the chicken and add it to the reduced stock. Cook, stirring constantly, over low heat until the stock has thickened. Remove the mixture from the heat and add the chopped pimientos.

Divide the pastry in half. Roll out half and line a 9-inch pie pan. Trim, leaving ½-inch of the pastry over the edge. Roll the remaining dough for the top crust. Prick with a fork. Pour the chicken mixture into the pie pan. Fit the top crust over the filling and trim it even with the under crust. Turn under the edges of the pastry and pinch closed. Cut slits into the crust to allow steam to escape. Bake at 400° for 30 minutes.

Makes 6 to 8 servings.

Main Dishes

ne-dish Chicken

1 head broccoli, cut into spears
6 boneless chicken breasts
1 10½-ounce can condensed golden
mushroom soup

1 cup shredded Monterey Jack
cheese

■ In the bottom of a casserole dish arrange the broccoli spears. Arrange the chicken in a single layer over the broccoli. Spoon the soup over the chicken. Bake at 375° for 45 minutes. Remove the cover and strain the excess fat. Sprinkle the cheese over the top. Return the dish to the oven and bake for about 10 minutes more, until the cheese is melted.

Makes 4 to 6 servings.

ᎬLVIS brought his father and grandmother to Germany. He tried to make a normal life on the base. His house was furnished just like an American home, with television sets, a piano, and a refrigerator stocked with hamburger meat, beans, and Brown 'n' Serve rolls.

*𝒮*our Cream Chicken

1 4-pound roasting chicken
¼ cup all-purpose flour
1 tablespoon paprika
1 teaspoon salt

¼ cup butter
1 large onion, sliced
2 cups hot water
1 cup sour cream

■ Remove the bones from the chicken and cut it into serving pieces. Blend the flour with paprika and salt. Coat the chicken pieces in the flour mixture.

In a skillet melt the butter. Brown the chicken. Add the onions at the last stage of the frying process. Cook until the chicken is soft. Add the remaining flour, blending with the drippings from the chicken. Slowly add the water, blending until smooth.

Cover and simmer for 1½ hours. Add the sour cream and simmer for 5 minutes more.

Makes 6 servings.

☆ **ELVIS in a publicity photo**

C hicken Livers with Mushrooms

¼ **pound chicken livers**	1½ **cups sliced mushrooms**
1 **teaspoon salt**	1 **cup chicken broth**
¼ **cup all-purpose flour**	1 **cup milk**
¼ **cup butter**	**Pepper to taste**
1 **onion, chopped**	**Toast**

■ Wash the chicken livers in cold water. Drain and pat dry. Place the livers on top of waxed paper. Sprinkle with salt and half the flour to coat. In a skillet melt the butter and sauté the onions for 3 minutes. Add the livers and cook until lightly browned on the bottom. Turn the livers and add the mushrooms. Push to one side of the skillet. Blend the remaining flour into the fat. Slowly add the broth, milk, and pepper. Cook for 5 minutes stirring to keep smooth. When the sauce thickens, blend in the livers and mushrooms. Serve over toast.

Makes 4 servings.

Main Dishes

145

C ornish Game Hens

2 game hens	**1 cup light cream**
1 lemon	**1½ cups green grapes**
Salt to taste	**1½ cups butter**

■ Rub the game hens with the juice of half a lemon. Sprinkle salt on the inside and outside of each bird. Move the oven rack to the lowest position. Place the hens in a shallow pan. Mix 2 tablespoons of lemon juice with 2 tablespoons of the cream and spoon some of the mixture into each cavity. Skewer the cavities shut. Bake at 375° for 1 hour. After 30 and 40 minutes, baste with whipping cream. After 50 minutes, pour the remaining cream over the hens.

Remove the hens to a serving platter when done. Stir the pan juices to blend. Pour into a sauce dish. In a skillet melt the butter and lightly sauté the grapes. Arrange the grapes around the hens and serve at once.

Makes 2 servings.

C hicken & Squash

2½ pounds acorn squash	**1 teaspoon salt**
¼ cup butter	**Pepper to taste**
⅓ cup all-purpose flour	**1½ cups diced chicken**
2 cups milk	

■ Slice the squash lengthwise. Scrape out the seeds and pulp. Rub the cut edges with butter. Place the squash halves cut-side down in a baking pan. Bake at 400° for 50 minutes or until the squash is soft on the inside.

In a saucepan melt the butter and blend in the flour and milk. Cook until it boils and becomes thick, stirring constantly to keep it smooth. Add the seasonings and diced chicken. Simmer over low heat until hot. Remove the squash to a serving platter. Pour the creamed chicken into the hollowed squash. Scoop out the squash along with the creamed chicken.

Makes 6 servings.

Fit For a King

☆ WEARING his famous gold suit during the
Singer Special in 1968

tuffed Chicken

1 6¾-ounce package wild rice
Oil
1 4-pound chicken, giblets and liver
   reserved

½ pound fresh mushrooms, sliced
1 green bell pepper, sliced
1 medium onion, chopped

■ Prepare the rice according to the package directions. In a skillet heat the oil and sauté the giblets, liver, mushrooms, pepper, and onion until tender. When the giblets and liver are done, chop them into small pieces and return them to the mushroom mixture. Add the cooked rice. Stuff the chicken with the rice mixture and place it on a spit. Cook the chicken until done.

   Makes 6 servings.

Main Dishes

𝒞 hicken Pancakes

2 teaspoons butter
½ cup finely diced celery
3 tablespoons finely chopped onion
¼ cup chicken gravy
1½ cups cooked and finely chopped
   chicken
Salt and pepper to taste

2 cups canned tomatoes
Dash chili powder
4 teaspoons sugar
Dash salt
Dash cayenne pepper
4 freshly baked 6-inch pancakes

■ In a skillet melt the butter and sauté the celery and onion for about 3 minutes. Blend in the gravy and stir until smooth and thick. Add the chicken. Season with salt and pepper. Keep the chicken mixture hot.

In a saucepan combine the tomatoes, chili powder, sugar, salt, and cayenne pepper. Cook rapidly until the liquid has almost evaporated and the tomatoes have thickened.

Spoon hot chicken along the center of each pancake and roll up. Pour the tomato sauce over each.

Makes 4 servings.

𝒞 rispy Fried Chicken

1 cup pancake mix
Salt to taste
¾ cup water

1 2-pound fryer chicken, cut into
   serving pieces
Oil

■ In a mixing bowl combine the pancake mix with the salt and water. Beat 3 minutes to blend. Dip the chicken in the batter and drain off the excess batter.

Deep fry the chicken in hot oil (350°) for 10 minutes or until golden brown. Drain on paper towels.

Makes 4 servings.

C hicken Stew

½ cup chopped celery leaves
½ cup chopped parsley
1 teaspoon tarragon
1 teaspoon allspice
¼ teaspoon cinnamon

Salt and pepper to taste
3 tablespoons olive oil
6 whole chicken legs
1½ cups white wine

■ In a large mixing bowl blend all of the ingredients except the olive oil, chicken, and wine. Coat a large casserole dish with the olive oil. Layer ⅓ of the chicken in the dish, and top with ⅓ of the dry ingredients. Repeat twice. Pour the wine over all. Bake at 375° for 1 hour and 15 minutes.

Makes 4 servings.

S outhwest Barbecued Chicken

1 cup ketchup
5 tablespoons unsalted butter
¼ cup strong coffee
3 tablespoons Worcestershire sauce
2 tablespoons crushed red chiles

1 tablespoon packed dark brown
  sugar
Salt to taste
1 4-pound chicken, cut into serving
  pieces

■ In a saucepan combine all of the ingredients except the chicken. Simmer uncovered over medium heat for 15 minutes. Place the chicken in a shallow pan. Pour the sauce over the chicken and let it marinate for 2 hours.

Prepare the barbecue grill. When the fire is ready, cover the rack with a layer of heavy-duty aluminum foil. Puncture to create ventilation. Position the rack 5 inches above the heat source.

Place the chicken on the rack, skin-side up. Cover the grill. Cook chicken slowly, basting frequently with the sauce. Turn the pieces after 30 minutes. Continue cooking and basting the chicken for 40 more minutes or until tender and smoky. Serve it with the remaining sauce.

Makes 8 servings.

Main Dishes

149

reamed Chicken in Pastry Shells

2 tablespoons butter
½ cup sliced mushrooms
2 tablespoons finely chopped
   onions
¼ cup chopped green bell pepper
½ cup milk

2½ cups condensed cream of chicken
   soup
Salt and pepper to taste
2½ cups diced cooked chicken
  8 4-inch prebaked pastry shells

■ In a saucepan melt the butter. Add the mushrooms, onion, and pepper, and sauté until the onion is transparent. Add the milk and the cream of chicken soup. Season with salt and pepper. Blend in the chicken and heat through but do not boil. Spoon the hot mixture into the pastry shells.

Makes 8 servings.

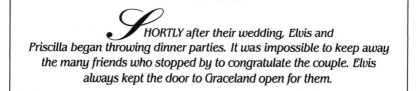

HORTLY after their wedding, Elvis and Priscilla began throwing dinner parties. It was impossible to keep away the many friends who stopped by to congratulate the couple. Elvis always kept the door to Graceland open for them.

hicken à la King

1 10-ounce package frozen peas
⅓ cup butter
½ pound mushrooms, sliced
¼ cup all-purpose flour
½ teaspoon salt
Pepper to taste

1½ cups chicken broth
1½ cups cream
 1 2-ounce can pimiento strips
 3 cups chopped cooked chicken
Buttered toast

■ Cook the peas according to the package directions. In a saucepan melt the butter and sauté the mushrooms until tender. Remove the mushrooms and set them aside. Stir the flour, salt, and pepper into the butter, blending until smooth. Heat until the mixture bubbles and thickens, about 4 minutes. Slowly add the chicken broth, cream, and pimiento strips. Cook until thickened. Add the chicken, peas, and mushrooms. Cook, stirring constantly, for 5 minutes or until the chicken is heated through. Pour the mixture over buttered toast.

Makes 4 servings.

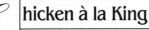

$\mathscr{B}$ arbecue Beef Kabobs

¼ cup butter
1 medium onion, chopped
1 8-ounce can tomato sauce
¼ cup chili sauce
⅓ cup red wine vinegar
1 tablespoon spicy mustard
2 tablespoons Worcestershire sauce
¼ cup packed light brown sugar

Salt and pepper to taste
2 pounds round steak, cut into
  1-inch cubes
12 cherry tomatoes
12 small white onions
1 green bell pepper, cut into 1-inch
  pieces
Fresh mushrooms

■ In a saucepan melt the butter and sauté the onions until tender. Add the tomato sauce, chili sauce, vinegar, mustard, Worcestershire sauce, brown sugar, salt, and pepper. Cover and simmer for 30 minutes.

Alternately place cubes of beef, tomatoes, onions, pepper pieces, and mushrooms on skewers. Place the skewers in a shallow pan. Pour the sauce over the skewers and refrigerate them overnight.

Grill the kabobs for 6 to 8 minutes, brushing frequently with the sauce.

Makes 4.

☆ WITH Priscilla, Lisa Marie, and Charles Hodges

Main Dishes

151

$\mathscr{S}$ paghetti & Meatballs

1 pound spaghetti	½ pound ground beef
3 tablespoons butter	½ pound ground pork
½ cup chopped onion	1 cup bread crumbs
1 clove garlic, minced	1 tablespoon finely chopped parsley
3½ cups canned tomatoes	1 egg, beaten
1 6-ounce can tomato paste	Salt and pepper to taste
1 teaspoon salt	2 tablespoons all-purpose flour
Pepper to taste	3 tablespoons butter
Oregano to taste	¼ cup grated Parmesan cheese

■ Prepare the spaghetti according to the package directions. In a skillet melt 3 tablespoons of butter and sauté the onion and garlic until transparent. Remove the skillet from the heat and add the tomatoes, tomato paste, salt, pepper, and oregano. Simmer for 1 hour.

In a mixing bowl combine the ground beef and ground pork. Blend in the bread crumbs, parsley, egg, salt, and pepper. Shape the meat mixture into 1-inch balls. Roll the meatballs in the flour. Melt 3 tablespoons of butter in a large skillet over medium heat and brown the meatballs. Drain the fat from the skillet. Pour the sauce over the meatballs, cover, and simmer over low heat for 20 minutes.

Toss the sauce and meatballs with the spaghetti. Place the spaghetti on a serving platter and top with Parmesan cheese.

Makes 4 servings.

$\mathscr{S}$ tuffed Ham Slices

2 smoked ham slices, each 1-inch thick	¼ cup packed light brown sugar
	½ teaspoon dry mustard
4 cups bread crumbs	⅓ cup butter, melted
½ cup seedless raisins	6 slices pineapple, with syrup

■ Place the ham slices in a 13 x 8-inch baking pan. In a bowl mix all of the ingredients except the pineapple slices. Toss thoroughly and spoon over the ham. Place a pineapple slice in each corner of the baking dish. Cut the remaining slices into wedges and arrange them on top of the ham. Bake at 300° for 1 hour and 30 minutes. Baste with the reserved pineapple juice.

Makes 2 servings.

Fit For a King

$\mathscr{S}$ autéed Sausage with Peppers

1¼ pounds Italian sausage, cut into
   1-inch pieces
1 onion, sliced
1 red bell pepper, cut into strips
½ cup black olives, cut in half

2 cloves garlic, minced
¼ cup vermouth
2 tablespoons basil
Cooked rice

■ In a skillet brown the sausage. Remove the sausage from the skillet. Separate the onion slices into rings and place them in the skillet. Sauté the onions in the sausage drippings for 2 minutes. Add the pepper, olives, and garlic. Cook for 2 minutes more. Return the sausage to the pan, and add the vermouth. Cook on high until the liquid is reduced by half. Remove the skillet from the heat and stir in the basil. Serve over cooked rice.

Makes 4 to 6 servings.

☆ ELVIS'S first starring role was in *Love Me Tender*
with Debra Paget.

Main Dishes

$\mathscr{B}$ eef Stroganoff

3 quarts water	⅓ cup butter
1 tablespoon salt	½ cup finely chopped onion
2 cups elbow macaroni	1 clove garlic, minced
½ cup all-purpose flour	1 cup beef broth
½ teaspoon salt	1 tablespoon sherry
Pepper to taste	1 cup sour cream
2 pounds round steak, cut ¼-inch thick	1 teaspoon Worcestershire sauce

■ In a large saucepan boil the water with the salt. Add the macaroni and boil uncovered for 15 minutes. Drain. Rinse with hot water and set aside. Cut the round steak into 2 x ½-inch strips. In a mixing bowl combine the flour, salt, and pepper. Coat the meat in the flour mixture.

In a heavy skillet melt the butter. Add the meat strips, onion, and garlic. Cook over medium heat, browning the meat evenly on all sides. Add the beef broth and sherry, and bring the liquid to a boil. Reduce the heat, cover, and simmer for 20 minutes.

In a small bowl blend together the sour cream and Worcestershire sauce. When the meat is tender, remove it from the skillet. Blend in the sour cream and Worcestershire sauce a little at a time, stirring constantly. Return the skillet to the heat. Continue cooking over very low heat, stirring constantly, for 3 minutes. Place the macaroni on a serving platter. Top with the stroganoff.

Makes 4 servings.

$\mathscr{E}$LVIS entertained the way folks did
back home: easy conversation, a good stock of food
(including chocolate milk and junk food), music, and television.
Those were the basic ingredients of an Elvis get-together.
He preferred this to the loud, crowded parties he was
always asked to attend. He enjoyed himself best when
surrounded by his own friends on his own terms.

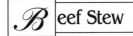

2 pounds flank steak	Boiling water
All-purpose flour	4 medium potatoes, peeled and
Salt and pepper to taste	quartered
1 medium onion, sliced	4 carrots, diced
3 tablespoons drippings	4 turnips, diced

■ Cut the meat into 1-inch cubes. In a mixing bowl blend the flour with the salt and pepper. Coat the meat in the flour mixture. In a stew pot melt the drippings. Brown the meat until done. Add the sliced onion and enough boiling water to cover. Place a lid only part way over the pot. Simmer slowly for 2 to 3 hours or until the meat is tender.

About 30 minutes before the stew is done add the potatoes, carrots, and turnips. To thicken the gravy blend equal amounts of flour and water. Slowly blend the mixture into the stew until smooth. Let the gravy cook for several minutes to thicken.

Makes 6 servings.

☆ IN *That's the Way It Is* in 1970

Main Dishes

*T*urkey with Stuffing & Gravy

8 cups soft bread cubes	1 12-pound ready-to-cook turkey
1½ teaspoons salt	2 teaspoons salt
1 teaspoon sage	1 cup butter, melted
¾ cup milk	2 cups chicken broth
⅓ cup chopped celery	½ cup water
⅓ cup chopped onion	¼ cup all-purpose flour
¼ teaspoon pepper	¼ teaspoon salt
¾ cup butter, melted	Pepper to taste

■ In a large bowl combine the bread cubes, salt, and sage. Blend in the milk, celery, onion, pepper, and ¾ cup of melted butter. Toss thoroughly. Wash and dry the turkey. Rub the cavity with salt. Place the turkey breast-side up on the rack of a roasting pan. Spoon the stuffing into the cavity of the turkey and skewer the opening shut. Place any remaining stuffing in a baking dish. Brush the turkey with the remaining melted butter. Bake the turkey at 325° for 4 hours or until a meat thermometer registers 190°. Baste occasionally during baking. Let the turkey cool for 30 minutes. Bake any remaining stuffing at 350° for about 20 minutes.

In a saucepan bring the chicken broth to a boil. In a blender mix the water and flour until smooth. Slowly pour half of the flour mixture into the broth. Return the mixture to a boil. Add the remaining flour mixture as needed for the desired thickness. Season with salt and pepper. Serve the gravy with the turkey.

Makes 8 to 12 servings.

*S*tuffed Breast of Lamb

1 lamb breast	½ cup diced celery
1 teaspoon salt	1 teaspoon chopped onion
1 teaspoon pepper	2 tablespoons melted butter
2 cups soft bread crumbs	¼ cup beef stock

■ Wipe the lamb breast clean. Rub the surface with half of the salt and pepper. In a mixing bowl combine the remaining ingredients. Coat the skin side of the breast. Roll up and tie securely.

Place the rolled breast in a baking pan. Add water, cover, and bake at 325° for 45 minutes per pound of meat. Uncover and bake for 30 minutes. Drain off the excess fat.

Makes 6 servings.

Fit For a King

☆ **ELVIS with fans**

*WHEN Elvis was at Graceland,
he would often go down to the front gates to visit with his fans.
When he was in Hollywood or on the road, his fans were
allowed to get a peek at the King's mansion.
Armed with cameras, they took pictures of the grounds. Once inside
the house, they could see his music room, trophy room, and den. And,
of course, everyone's favorite room was the kitchen.*

☆ **MEETING fans backstage after a concert**

ℐ teak Julienne

4 teaspoons garlic butter
½ teaspoon Worcestershire sauce
4 steak fillets
Dijon mustard
4 cups sliced mushrooms

Brandy
Demi-glacé
1 cup heavy cream
1 cup red wine

■ In a saucepan melt the garlic butter over medium heat. Brush Worcestershire sauce over each fillet and spread mustard over each. Sear the fillets in the garlic butter over medium-low heat. Turn the fillets and baste, mixing the butter with the mustard. Add the sliced mushrooms. Increase the heat to medium-high. When the steaks are sizzling, turn them and add the brandy. Ignite the brandy and flambé the steaks. When the flame subsides, add the demi-glacé, heavy cream, and red wine. Sauté until the sauce thickens. Serve immediately.

Makes 4 servings.

Fit For a King

158

$\mathcal{M}$aple Spareribs

3 pounds lean spareribs, trimmed
of all excess fat
½ cup mustard
1 cup cold water
½ cup tomato purée
½ cup maple syrup

¼ cup apple cider vinegar
½ cup finely chopped onions
¼ cup Worcestershire sauce
½ teaspoon Tabasco sauce
1½ teaspoons salt
½ teaspoon ground black pepper

■ Preheat the broiler. Pat the spareribs completely dry and cut them in half. Brush them thoroughly with mustard. Layer the ribs fat-side up on the rack of a broiler pan. Broil 4 inches from the heat for 5 minutes. Turn the ribs meat side up and broil them about 5 minutes longer.

Remove the ribs from the pan. Discard all of the fat that accumulated and pour the water into the broiler pan. Return the ribs to the pan.

In a bowl combine the tomato purée, ¼ cup of maple syrup, vinegar, onion, Worcestershire sauce, Tabasco, salt, and pepper. Mix well. Add the remaining maple syrup.

With a pastry brush, spread ¼ cup of the sauce over the ribs. Reduce the oven temperature to 350°. Lower the oven rack and place the ribs in the middle of the oven. Bake them for 1 hour or until the ribs are brown and crisp. Baste the ribs with the sauce every 15 minutes.

Makes 4 servings.

$\mathcal{L}$ISA MARIE told a reporter from Life magazine, "There's just an incredible feeling about that house even now that it's open to the public. I go there three or four times a year. At night when we're alone in the house and the same maids are cooking corn bread and black-eyed peas for us like they always did—it feels just the way it used to, when my dad was alive."

C ranberry Roast Pork

1 4-pound boneless pork roast, tied
with string
Salt and black pepper to taste
¾ cup fresh orange juice
¼ teaspoon cinnamon
¼ teaspoon ginger
1 16-ounce can whole sweetened
cranberries
¼ cup chopped onion

■ Rub the roast with salt and pepper. Place the roast on a rack in a broiler pan. Bake at 325° for 2 hours and 30 minutes to 3 hours, or until a meat thermometer registers 175°.

In a saucepan combine the remaining ingredients. Bring the mixture to a boil. Remove the sauce from the heat. Halfway through baking the roast, begin basting it every 15 minutes with the cranberry mixture. The remaining sauce may be served with the sliced pork.

Makes 6 servings.

B eef Burgundy

2 tablespoons soy sauce
2 tablespoons all-purpose flour
2 pounds beef stew meat, cubed
4 medium carrots, peeled and
cut into chunks
2 large onions, sliced
1 cup thinly sliced celery
2 large cloves garlic, minced
Black pepper to taste
¼ teaspoon marjoram
¼ teaspoon thyme
1 cup dry red wine
1½ cups sliced mushrooms
Steamed rice

■ In a mixing bowl blend the soy sauce with the flour. Add the beef to the soy sauce mixture and toss to coat. In a Dutch oven combine the meat, carrots, onions, celery, garlic, pepper, marjoram, thyme, and wine. Stir gently to mix. Seal the top with foil. Place the lid over the foil and then place a second layer of foil over the lid. Fold the foil around the sides of the pot. Cover tightly and bake at 325° for 1 hour.

Add the mushrooms, stirring gently. Cover and return to the oven. Continue to bake for 1 to 2 hours or until the meat and vegetables are tender. Serve over steamed rice.

Makes 4 servings.

Fit For a King

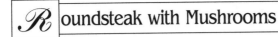oundsteak with Mushrooms

1 pound round steak, tenderized
Salt and pepper to taste
All-purpose flour
1 onion, minced

¼ cup minced parsley
1 cup beef stock
1 cup sliced mushrooms
¼ teaspoon paprika

■ Season the meat with salt and pepper, and coat it with flour. In a skillet brown the steak. Remove the steak from the skillet, and place it in a casserole dish. In the same skillet sauté the onion and parsley until the onion is tender. Add the beef stock and mushrooms, and heat through. Baste the steak with the gravy. Bake at 350° for 1 hour. Sprinkle paprika over the steak before serving.

Makes 2 servings.

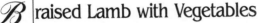raised Lamb with Vegetables

3 tablespoons all-purpose flour
½ teaspoon salt
1 pound boneless lamb shoulder,
   cut into 1-inch pieces
2 tablespoons drippings

1¼ cups water
1 medium eggplant, sliced
2 medium tomatoes, sliced
Salt and pepper to taste

■ In a mixing bowl combine the flour and salt. Coat the lamb pieces in the flour. In a skillet melt the drippings and brown the lamb. Add ½ cup of water. Cover and simmer for 1 hour, adding more water as needed.

Remove the cover and arrange the sliced eggplant and tomatoes over the lamb pieces. Sprinkle with salt and pepper. Cover and simmer for 20 minutes.

Makes 4 servings.

R oast Leg of Lamb

1 leg of lamb	**1 tablespoon crushed thyme**
1 tablespoon minced garlic	**Olive oil**
1 tablespoon crushed basil	**Water**
1 tablespoon crushed rosemary	

■ Cut the layers of fat from the roast in large pieces and reserve. In a mixing bowl blend the garlic and herbs with enough olive oil to double the volume. Brush the entire surface of the lamb with the herbed oil.

Carefully replace the fat on the roast. Cover the roast and let it stand for 1 hour. Place the roast, with the fat, in a roasting pan.

Roast uncovered at 400° for 20 minutes. Reduce the heat to 325° and add 2 cups of water to the bottom of the pan. Roast until the inner temperature registers 140° to 180°. Use the pan juices to make gravy if desired.

Makes 4 servings.

C orned Beef & Cabbage

2 pounds corned beef	**Vinegar**
1 large head cabbage, quartered	
4 medium potatoes, peeled and quartered	

■ Soak the corned beef in cold water for 1 hour. Drain and transfer the corned beef to a stew pot. Cover completely with cold water. Add 1 teaspoon of vinegar per quart of water. Add the potatoes. Cook slowly for 2 hours.

Place the cabbage in a separate pot of boiling water. Cook until tender. Drain.

To serve, place the corned beef on a platter and surround it with the cabbage and potatoes.

Makes 4 servings.

acon & Tomato Sandwiches

2 medium tomatoes, sliced　　　　**8 slices crisp bacon**
8 slices buttered bread

■ Arrange the sliced tomatoes on top of 4 slices of buttered bread. Place 2 strips of bacon on each sandwich. Top with the remaining bread slices. Cut the sandwiches diagonally.

　Mayonnaise may be substituted for butter, if desired.

　Makes 4 sandwiches.

☆ **IN THE 1968 Singer Special**

 eef & Potato Casserole

3 cups ground beef	**3 cups mashed potatoes**
2 tablespoons drippings	**1 cup milk**
2 tablespoons chopped onion	**Salt and pepper to taste**
1 tablespoon chopped parsley	**3 eggs, separated**

■ In a skillet brown the beef. Drain all but 2 tablespoons of drippings. Sauté the onions and parsley. In a large bowl combine the beef, potatoes, and milk. Season with salt and pepper.

In a mixing bowl beat the egg whites until stiff. In a separate bowl beat the egg yolks until thick. Blend the yolks into the beef mixture. Fold in the egg whites. Transfer the mixture to a well-greased casserole dish. Bake at 350° for 1 hour.

Makes 4 servings.

☆ **ELVIS smiles for the photographers.**

Rice & Sausage Casserole

¾ **pound pork sausage**
2 **tablespoons hot water**
1½ **cups cracker crumbs**
1½ **cups white rice, cooked**
1½ **cups canned tomatoes**
¼ **cup chopped green bell pepper**

3 **tablespoons minced celery leaves**
1¼ **tablespoons minced onion**
1¼ **teaspoons salt**
Pepper to taste
2 **tablespoons butter**

■ Cut the sausage into small serving pieces. In a skillet brown the sausage. Add the water, cracker crumbs, rice, tomatoes, pepper, celery leaves, and onion. Season with salt and pepper. Blend thoroughly.

Pour the mixture into a well-greased casserole dish and dot with butter. Bake at 375° for 30 minutes.

Makes 6 servings.

GLADYS never minded when Elvis brought a cousin or his friends over for a snack or to play in the front yard. She never seemed to mind the noise.

Cheese & Sweet Potato Casserole

2 **pounds sweet potatoes**
1 **cup boiling water**
½ **teaspoon salt**
Pepper to taste

1 **tablespoon sugar**
1 **cup milk**
¾ **cup grated sharp Cheddar cheese**
1 **tablespoon butter**

■ Scrub, peel, and slice the potatoes. Place them in a saucepan and add the boiling water and half the salt. Cover and boil for 15 minutes.

Grease a 5-cup casserole dish. Place a layer of potatoes in the bottom and sprinkle with salt, pepper, and sugar. Continue layering. Pour milk over the top. Cover with the grated cheese, and dot with butter. Bake at 375° for 30 minutes.

Makes 4 servings.

Main Dishes

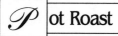ot Roast

5 pounds chuck roast
½ cup all-purpose flour
Salt and pepper to taste

1 onion, sliced
2 cups boiling water

Gravy
1 tablespoon butter

1 tablespoon all-purpose flour

■ Wipe the meat with a damp cloth. Blend ½ cup of flour with the salt and pepper. Season the chuck roast with the flour. In a Dutch oven brown the roast. Add the sliced onions. Slowly add the boiling water. Cover and simmer for 3 to 4 hours. Remove the roast to a hot platter.

In a saucepan melt the butter. Blend in the flour. Gradually add the pan juices, and cook until thickened. Thinly slice the roast. Serve it with the gravy.

Makes 6 servings.

ℰLVIS would spend most of his free time away from the New Frontier Hotel in Las Vegas at the local movie theater. He watched Western films mostly.
Back at the hotel, he would request from room service that a platter of peanut butter and banana sandwiches be sent up to his room.

℘eanut Butter & Banana Sandwiches

¼ cup creamy peanut butter
2 very ripe bananas

10 slices buttered bread
Butter

■ Blend the peanut butter with the banana until creamy. Spread the mixture over 5 slices of the bread. Top with the remaining bread.

In a skillet melt enough butter to coat the bottom of the pan. Place the sandwiches in the butter and grill them until the bread is lightly toasted. Flip to grill the other side. Drain on paper towels.

Makes 5 sandwiches.

Fit For a King

☆ **THINKING** about his answer during a press conference

Main Dishes

☆ **POSING with Dolores Hart and Jan Shepard at the casting party for** *King Creole*

T WAS hard to describe the real Elvis. A lot has been said and written about his unique musical talents, his boyish charm, and handsome good looks. He had a sincere, genuine concern for all people. And, typically Southern, he had good manners and held the respect of so many who met him. Elvis, the country boy who turned King of Rock 'n' Roll, was genuine. And it showed through in his music.

Fit For a King

$\mathscr{D}$ESSERTS

herry Angel Food Cake

1 cup cake flour	**1¼ teaspoons cream of tartar**
1½ cups sugar	**½ teaspoon vanilla extract**
10 egg whites	**½ teaspoon cherry extract**
¼ teaspoon salt	**¼ teaspoon almond extract**

■ Have the ingredients at room temperature. Into a mixing bowl sift the flour. Measure 1 cup and resift it 5 times with ¾ cup of sugar. In a large glass mixing bowl combine the egg whites, salt, and cream of tartar. Beat the egg whites until stiff. Slowly add the remaining sugar in 5 portions, beating after each addition. Beat in the vanilla, cherry, and almond extracts. Fold in the flour mixture in 5 portions, beating after each addition. Pour the batter into a 10-inch tube pan with a removable bottom. Cut the batter with a knife to break any air bubbles. Place the oven rack in the lowest position, and place the pan in the center. Bake at 300° for 1 hour or until the top is brown.

Remove the cake from the oven and invert the pan onto a funnel. Leave the cake upside down until cooled.

Makes 10 servings.

$\mathscr{F}$OR HIS VISIT with the Beatles, Elvis served a midnight supper. Included among the variety of southern dishes were broiled chicken livers, deviled eggs, and sweet and sour meatballs. The Beatles said that being with Elvis was the high point of their U.S. tour.

$\mathscr{P}$ ound Cake

1 cup butter, softened	4 eggs
1 cup sugar	2 cups cake flour
¼ teaspoon grated lemon rind	¼ teaspoon baking powder
1 teaspoon fresh lemon juice	

■ Grease and flour a 9 x 5-inch loaf pan. In a mixing bowl cream together the butter and sugar. Add the lemon rind, lemon juice, and eggs. Beat well. Add the cake flour and baking powder, and blend until smooth. Pour the batter into the baking pan. Bake at 300° for 1 hour and 15 minutes.

Let the cake cool before serving.

Makes 12 servings.

☆ AUDITIONING for *Love Me Tender*

$\mathcal{C}$ oconut Cake

1⅔ cups cake flour	⅓ cup coconut milk
1 cup sugar	¼ cup milk
¾ teaspoon salt	3 egg whites
3 teaspoons baking powder	1 teaspoon vanilla extract
⅓ cup plus 1 tablespoon shortening	3 cups grated coconut

■ Line the bottom of two 8-inch layer pans with waxed paper. Lightly grease the paper and sides of the pan. Have all of the ingredients at room temperature.

Into a bowl sift the cake flour. Add the sugar, salt, and baking powder, and resift 3 times. Add the shortening and coconut milk, and beat with an electric mixer at medium speed for 2 minutes. Scrape the sides of the bowl. Add the milk, egg whites, and vanilla. Beat 2 minutes more. Scrape the sides of the bowl frequently to keep the batter smooth.

Bake at 350° for 25 minutes. Remove the cake from the oven and let it stand for about 5 minutes. Remove it to cool thoroughly. Top with coconut, and stack the layers.

Makes 8 to 12 servings.

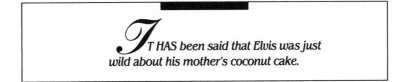

$\mathcal{I}$T HAS been said that Elvis was just wild about his mother's coconut cake.

$\mathcal{R}$ um Cake

1 18-ounce box yellow cake mix	1 teaspoon nutmeg
1 3-ounce box instant vanilla pudding mix	¾ cup rum
4 eggs	¾ cup oil

■ In a bowl combine the vanilla pudding and the cake mix. Add the eggs, nutmeg, rum, and oil. Beat with an electric mixer at low speed for 5 minutes. Pour the batter into a greased and floured tube pan. Bake at 350° for 50 minutes or until a toothpick inserted in the center comes out clean. Let the cake cool thoroughly before serving.

Makes 12 servings.

$\mathscr{A}$pplesauce Cake

1 cup butter
3½ cups applesauce
4 cups all-purpose flour
2 cups sugar
2 teaspoons salt

2 teaspoons baking soda
2 teaspoons cinnamon
1 teaspoon nutmeg
½ teaspoon allspice
2 cups chopped walnuts

Streusel Topping
¼ cup all-purpose flour
½ cup sugar
¼ cup cornflake crumbs

½ teaspoon cinnamon
2 tablespoons butter

■ Grease an 8 x 12-inch baking pan. In a large saucepan melt 1 cup of butter with the applesauce over medium heat. Stir occasionally. Remove the mixture from the heat.

Into a mixing bowl sift the 4 cups of flour, 2 cups of sugar, salt, baking soda, 2 teaspoons of cinnamon, nutmeg, and allspice. Fold the dry ingredients into the applesauce mixture. Blend thoroughly. Add the walnuts. Pour the batter into the prepared pan, spreading evenly.

In a small bowl combine the remaining ingredients. Add the butter and mix until crumbly. Sprinkle the streusel topping over the batter. Bake at 350° for 45 minutes.

Makes 12 servings.

$\mathscr{G}$inger-Peach Upside Down Cake

1 cup packed light brown sugar
6 tablespoons unsalted butter,
    melted
3 peaches
2½ cups all-purpose flour
2 teaspoons baking soda
½ teaspoon cinnamon
2 teaspoons ginger

¼ teaspoon salt
½ cup dark molasses
1 cup boiling water
1 cup safflower oil
1 cup sugar
2 eggs, lightly beaten
2 teaspoons grated orange rind
Whipping cream

Fit For a King

■ Butter the sides of a 10 x 3-inch springform pan. In a bowl blend the brown sugar with the melted butter. Spread the mixture evenly in the bottom of the prepared pan.

Peel and pit the peaches, and cut them into ½-inch slices. Arrange the slices close together in a circular shape over the sugar in the bottom of the pan. Into a mixing bowl sift together the flour, baking soda, cinnamon, ginger, and salt. Set aside. Combine the molasses and water in another bowl and set it aside. In a large bowl beat the safflower oil and sugar until light. Beat in the eggs and orange rind. Add the molasses mixture. Stir in the dry ingredients and beat until well blended.

Pour the batter into the peach-lined pan. Bake at 350° for 1 hour or until a toothpick inserted in the center comes out clean. Cover with aluminum foil if it begins to burn at the edges. Let the cake cool in the pan for 30 minutes. Invert the cake onto a serving platter. Allow the glaze to drip down the sides of the cake. Serve with whipping cream.

Makes 8 to 10 servings.

ponge Cake

1 cup cake flour	5 large eggs, separated
1 cup sugar	1 tablespoon fresh lemon juice
¼ teaspoon grated orange rind	½ teaspoon cream of tartar
1½ teaspoons fresh orange juice	¼ teaspoon salt
1 tablespoon water	

■ Into a mixing bowl sift the flour. Measure 1 cup and resift 3 times. In a separate bowl combine ½ cup of sugar, the orange rind, orange juice, water, and egg yolks. Beat until thick and light. Add the lemon juice and flour, stirring until well blended.

In a separate glass bowl beat the egg whites until foamy. Add the cream of tartar and salt, and beat until stiff. Add the remaining sugar, 2 tablespoons at a time. Fold the egg whites into the egg yolk mixture. Pour the batter into a greased 9-inch tube pan. Cut the batter with a knife to break any air bubbles. Bake at 325° for 1 hour or until done. Loosen the sides with a knife and remove the cake from the pan. Cool the cake before serving.

Makes 6 servings.

ream Cheese Pound Cake

1½ cups butter, softened
  1 8-ounce package cream cheese
  3 cups sugar
  6 eggs

3 cups sifted cake flour
2 tablespoons vanilla extract
Confectioners' sugar

■ In a mixing bowl beat the butter with the cream cheese with an electric mixer. Gradually add the sugar. Beat until light and fluffy, about 5 minutes. Add the eggs, one at a time, beating well after each addition. Add the flour and vanilla.

Pour the batter into a well greased 10-inch tube pan. Bake at 325° for 1 hour and 30 minutes or until a toothpick inserted in the center comes out clean. Let the cake cool in the pan for 10 minutes. Remove it and let it cool completely. Sprinkle with confectioners' sugar.

Makes 6 servings.

P oppy Seed Pound Cake

1 cup butter
3 cups packed light brown sugar
6 eggs
2 teaspoons vanilla extract

3 cups all-purpose flour
¼ teaspoon baking soda
½ teaspoon salt
⅓ cup poppy seeds

■ In a large bowl cream together the butter and sugar until light and fluffy. Add the eggs one at a time, beating well after each addition. Add the vanilla. In a separate bowl combine the flour, baking soda, and salt. Fold the dry ingredients into the creamed mixture. Stir in the poppy seeds. Pour the batter into a greased 10-inch tube pan. Bake at 325° for 1 hour and 30 minutes, or until a toothpick inserted in the center comes out clean. Cool the cake in the pan for 10 minutes. Remove it to a wire rack.

Makes 8 servings.

$\mathcal{C}$ hocolate Zucchini Cake

1 cup packed light brown sugar
½ cup sugar
½ cup butter
½ cup oil
3 eggs
1 teaspoon vanilla extract
½ cup buttermilk
2½ cups all-purpose flour

½ teaspoon allspice
½ teaspoon cinnamon
¼ teaspoon salt
2 teaspoons baking soda
¼ cup cocoa
3 small zucchini, peeled and grated
1 cup semisweet chocolate chips

■ In a large mixing bowl cream together the sugars, butter, and oil. Add the eggs, vanilla, and buttermilk. Mix together thoroughly. In a separate bowl measure the dry ingredients and sift them together. Fold the dry ingredients into the creamed mixture, stirring until well blended. Add the zucchini and mix again thoroughly.

Pour the batter into a greased and floured 9 x 13-inch baking pan. Sprinkle chocolate chips on top. Bake at 325° for 45 minutes. Let the cake cool before serving.

Makes 8 servings.

☆ A LIVE performance at the Las Vegas Hilton in 1969

Desserts

$\mathscr{C}$ hocolate Pound Cake

1 cup butter	½ teaspoon baking powder
½ cup shortening	½ cup cocoa powder
3 cups sugar	1½ cups milk
5 eggs	1 teaspoon vanilla extract
3 cups all-purpose flour	

■ In a mixing bowl cream the butter, shortening, and sugar. Add the eggs one at a time, beating well after each addition. Into a separate bowl sift together the dry ingredients. Fold the dry ingredients into the creamed mixture alternately with the milk. Add the vanilla. Pour the batter into a 10-inch tube pan. Bake at 325° for 1 hour and 30 minutes. Let the cake cool before serving.

Makes 8 servings.

$\mathscr{C}$ ocoa Bundt Cake

1⅔ cups all-purpose flour	2 eggs
1 teaspoon salt	½ cup shortening
1½ teaspoons baking soda	1½ cups buttermilk
1½ cups sugar	½ teaspoon vanilla extract
½ cup cocoa	

Chocolate Glaze

¼ cup water	1 cup semisweet chocolate chips
¼ cup sugar	

■ In a mixing bowl combine the flour, baking soda, salt, 1½ cups of sugar, and cocoa. Add the eggs, shortening, buttermilk, and vanilla. Beat with an electric mixer on low speed for 1 minute. Scrape the sides of the bowl. Beat on high speed for 3 minutes more. Pour the batter into a greased and floured bundt pan. Bake at 350° for 50 minutes. Let the cake cool for 10 minutes, then remove the cake from the pan and place it on a wire rack to cool completely.

In a saucepan bring the water to a boil. Add the sugar and stir to dissolve. Remove the pan from the heat and add the chocolate chips, whisking until the chocolate is melted. Cool until slightly thickened. Drizzle the glaze over the cooled cake.

Makes 8 servings.

Fit For a King

ocoa Praline Cake

½ cup butter
1 cup buttermilk
2 cups packed light brown sugar
2 eggs
2 cups all-purpose flour

1 teaspoon baking soda
3 tablespoons cocoa
½ teaspoon salt
1 tablespoon vanilla extract

Icing
½ cup butter
1 cup packed light brown sugar

⅓ cup evaporated milk
1 cup chopped pecans

■ In a saucepan heat ½ cup of butter and the buttermilk until the butter is melted. Pour the mixture into a mixing bowl and add 2 cups of brown sugar and the eggs. Beat well. Into a separate bowl sift together the dry ingredients. Add the dry ingredients to the buttermilk mixture, blending until smooth. Add the vanilla. Pour the batter into a greased and floured 9 x 13-inch baking pan. Bake at 350° for 25 minutes.

In a separate saucepan combine ½ cup of butter, 1 cup of brown sugar, the evaporated milk, and pecans. Heat until the butter melts. Spread the icing over the cake while it is still warm. Place the cake under the broiler, about 4 inches away from the heat. Broil until the icing turns light brown, about 1 to 2 minutes.

Makes 8 servings.

ELVIS felt a strong obligation to his family and friends, not to mention his fans. Their loyalty meant the world to him. He always said that if it were possible he would have them all over to Graceland for a party. "If they are here to see me, they must be important."

$\mathcal{T}$ ennessee Jam Cake

2 squares unsweetened chocolate	**2 eggs, separated**
1½ cups sifted cake flour	**¾ cup buttermilk**
1½ teaspoons baking soda	**2 tablespoons whiskey**
¼ teaspoon salt	**½ cup seedless blackberry jam**
1 teaspoon allspice	**½ cup red raspberry jam**
¼ teaspoon cinnamon	**½ cup raisins**
⅓ cup butter	**½ cup currants**
½ cup sugar	**½ cup chopped walnuts**
½ cup packed light brown sugar	**Confectioners' sugar**

■ In a saucepan melt the chocolate and let it cool. In a bowl add the flour, baking soda, salt, allspice, and cinnamon. In a bowl cream the butter and add the sugars. Add the egg yolks, buttermilk, and whiskey alternately with the flour, beginning and ending with the flour. Add the jams and chocolate. Mix well.

Fold in the raisins, currants, and nuts. In a small bowl beat the egg whites until stiff. Fold in the batter. Pour the batter into a greased and floured 9-inch tube pan.

Bake at 350° for about 55 minutes. Let the cake cool in the pan for 10 minutes. Remove the cake to a cooling rack. Once cool, wrap it in aluminum foil. Store the cake in the refrigerator for 2 days. Top with confectioners' sugar.

Makes 8 servings.

$\mathcal{C}$ hocolate Oatmeal Cake

⅔ cup semisweet chocolate chips	**½ cup butter, softened**
1 cup oats	**1 cup sugar**
1¼ cups boiling water	**1 cup packed light brown sugar**
1½ cups all-purpose flour	**3 eggs, room temperature**
1 teaspoon baking soda	**1 teaspoon vanilla extract**

Topping

6 tablespoons butter, softened	**½ cup milk**
1 cup packed light brown sugar	**1½ cups flaked coconut**

Fit For a King

178

■ In a mixing bowl toss together the chocolate chips and oats. Pour the boiling water over the mixture and let it stand for 20 minutes.

In a separate bowl combine the flour and baking soda. In a large bowl cream together ½ cup of butter, the sugar, and 1 cup of brown sugar with an electric mixer at medium speed until fluffy. Add the eggs and vanilla, beating well. Fold in the oat mixture. Add the flour and blend well. Pour the batter into a greased and floured 9 x 13-inch pan. Bake at 350° for 40 minutes or until a toothpick inserted in the center comes out clean.

In a small mixing bowl cream together the butter and brown sugar with an electric mixer. Add the milk and blend well. Stir in the coconut with a spoon. Spread the topping over the hot cake. Return the cake to the oven for 4 minutes, making sure that it does not burn. Serve warm.

Makes 10 servings.

uttermilk Gingerbread

1½ cups all-purpose flour	½ cup butter, softened
½ teaspoon baking soda	½ cup sugar
½ teaspoon cinnamon	1 egg
¾ teaspoon ginger	½ cup molasses
½ teaspoon allspice	½ cup plus 2 tablespoons buttermilk
Salt to taste	

■ Line the bottom of an 8-inch square baking pan with waxed paper. Lightly grease the paper and the sides of the pan.

Into a bowl sift the flour. Measure 1½ cups and resift 3 times with the baking soda, cinnamon, ginger, allspice, and salt. With an electric mixer cream the butter. Add the sugar and egg, and beat until fluffy. Add the molasses and beat for 2 minutes. Add the flour mixture alternately with the buttermilk, beginning and ending with the flour. Beat after each addition.

Pour the batter into the prepared pan. Bake at 350° for 25 minutes. Let the gingerbread cool in the pan for about 5 minutes. Turn it out on a rack. Peel off the wax paper and invert.

Makes 8 servings.

☆ TAKING time out to sign autographs in a hallway of the Las Vegas Hilton

maretto Cheesecake

1½ cups graham cracker crumbs
2 tablespoons sugar
1 teaspoon cinnamon
¼ cup plus 2 tablespoons butter,
 melted

3 8-ounce packages cream cheese,
 softened
1 cup sugar
3 eggs
⅓ cup amaretto liqueur

Topping
1 cup sour cream
1 tablespoon plus 1 teaspoon
 sugar

1 tablespoon amaretto liqueur
¼ cup sliced toasted almonds
1 1½-ounce chocolate bar, grated

Fit For a King

■ In a mixing bowl combine the graham cracker crumbs, 2 tablespoons of sugar, cinnamon, and butter. Mix well. Press the mixture into the bottom and sides of a 9-inch springform pan. In a large bowl beat the cream cheese with 1 cup of sugar, mixing well. Add the eggs one at a time, beating well after each addition. Stir in ⅓ cup of amaretto. Pour the filling into the crust. Bake at 375° for 45 minutes or until set.

In a separate bowl combine the sour cream, sugar, and 1 tablespoon of amaretto. Stir well and spoon the mixture over the cheesecake. Bake at 500° for 5 minutes. Let the cheesecake cool, and then refrigerate it for 24 hours. Garnish with almonds and grated chocolate before serving.

Makes 8 to 10 servings.

ℭ hocolate Chip Cheesecake

3 tablespoons butter	1½ cups sour cream
20 chocolate wafers, crumbled	2 teaspoons vanilla extract
2 tablespoons sugar	1 cup semisweet chocolate chips
4 8-ounce packages cream cheese	1 8-ounce bar semisweet chocolate,
1 cup sugar	melted
4 large eggs	1 8-ounce bar semisweet chocolate

■ In a saucepan melt the butter. Remove the pan from the heat and add the crushed cookies and 2 tablespoons of sugar. Press the mixture evenly in the bottom of an oiled 9-inch springform pan. Freeze the crust until needed.

In a large mixing bowl beat the cream cheese and 1 cup of sugar with an electric mixer until smooth. Add the eggs, 2 at a time, beating after each addition. Blend in the sour cream, vanilla, chocolate chips, and melted chocolate. Pour the mixture into the crust. Lightly tap the pan on the counter to break any large air bubbles. Place the pan on a square of heavy aluminum foil. Wrap the foil around the sides of the pan. Place the springform pan in a larger pan, and add 2 inches of water to the larger pan. Bake at 275° for 1 hour to 1 hour and 30 minutes, until the center of the cake begins to feel firm. Remove the foil and place the pan on a wire rack to cool. Let the cheesecake cool for about 45 minutes. Refrigerate it for 5 hours before serving.

Heat the remaining bar of chocolate until it feels soft. Peel it with a vegetable peeler to make chocolate curls. Sprinkle the curls over the finished cheesecake.

Makes 6 servings.

Desserts

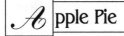pple Pie

**8 medium apples, peeled, and
  quartered**
1 tablespoon all-purpose flour
Salt to taste

¾ cup sugar
Pastry for 1 9-inch 2-crust pie
1 tablespoon butter
¼ teaspoon cinnamon

■ Slice the quartered apples lengthwise and set them aside.

In a mixing bowl blend the flour, salt, and sugar. Sprinkle half of the mixture in the bottom of the pie crust. Toss the apples with the remaining flour mixture. Arrange the slices close together in the bottom of the pie shell. Dot with butter. Sprinkle with cinnamon. Moisten the edge of the lower crust. Top with the remaining pastry. Press down gently around the edges to seal. Trim off the excess dough. Poke with a fork for ventilation.

Bake at 400° for 15 minutes. Reduce the heat to 325° and continue baking for 35 minutes. The apples will be tender and juice should be bubbling out of the air vents. Remove the pie to a wire rack and let it cool for 3 hours.

Makes 6 servings.

S hoo Fly Pie

2 8-inch pie crusts, unbaked
1 cup molasses
1 cup warm water
1 teaspoon baking soda
2 cups all-purpose flour

¼ teaspoon salt
½ cup sugar
¼ cup shortening
¾ teaspoon baking soda

■ In a large bowl beat the molasses, warm water, and 1 teaspoon of baking soda until foamy. In a separate bowl combine the flour, salt, sugar, and ¾ teaspoon of baking soda. Blend in the shortening with a fork until the mixture resembles coarse crumbs. Pour some of the molasses mixture into each pie shell, reserving the rest. Sprinkle a layer of the crumb mixture over the molasses in each pie shell. Top with the remaining molasses mixture, and sprinkle with the remaining crumb mixture. Bake at 350° for 45 minutes.

Makes 16 servings.

Fit For a King

182

$\mathscr{S}$outhern Pecan Pie

1 9-inch single pie crust, unbaked
4 eggs, lightly beaten
⅔ cup packed dark brown sugar
1⅓ cups light corn syrup
¼ cup unsalted butter, melted

½ teaspoon salt
4 teaspoons all-purpose flour
2 teaspoons vanilla extract
1½ cups coarsely chopped pecans

■ Bake the pie crust at 400° for 10 minutes or until it is set but not browned. Remove the crust and set it aside. Reduce the oven temperature to 375°.

In a large bowl combine the eggs, brown sugar, corn syrup, butter, salt, flour, and vanilla. Stir to blend. Add the pecans, and pour the mixture into the partially baked pie shell. Bake at 400° for about 35 minutes. Cover the edges of the crust with strips of foil if necessary to prevent excessive browning. Cool on a wire rack.

Makes 6 servings.

$\mathscr{G}$LADYS loved Elvis's friends. She would greet them with her wonderful southern hospitality. When a group of them stopped by to visit, she could be found in the kitchen cutting them a piece of freshly baked apple pie or a slice of coconut cake.

$\mathscr{C}$hocolate Pecan Pie

1½ cups coarsely chopped pecans
1 6-ounce package semisweet
  chocolate chips
1 8-inch pie crust, partially baked

½ cup light corn syrup
½ cup sugar
2 extra large eggs
¼ cup butter, melted and cooled

■ Sprinkle pecans and chocolate chips in the bottom of the partially baked pie shell. In a bowl blend the corn syrup, sugar, and eggs. Add the melted butter. Pour the mixture into the pie shell. Bake at 325° for about 1 hour.

Makes 8 servings.

Desserts

P raline Pumpkin Pie

⅓ cup finely chopped pecans
⅓ cup packed light brown sugar
2 tablespoons butter, softened
1 9-inch pie crust, unbaked
1 cup canned pumpkin
3 eggs
1½ cups heavy cream
½ cup packed light brown sugar

½ teaspoon salt
1 teaspoon cinnamon
¼ teaspoon cloves
¼ teaspoon ginger
¼ cup rum
2 egg whites
3 tablespoons sugar

■ In a small bowl blend the pecans with ⅓ cup of brown sugar and the butter. Spoon the mixture into the bottom of the pie shell and press gently with a spoon.

In a large bowl combine the pumpkin, 3 eggs, cream, ½ cup of brown sugar, salt, cinnamon, cloves, ginger, and rum. Blend well. Pour the filling into the pie shell. Bake at 400° for about 50 minutes.

In a separate bowl beat the egg whites until stiff, gradually adding the sugar while beating. Remove the pie from the oven and cover it with the meringue. Return the pie to the oven, increase the temperature to 425°, and bake until the meringue is lightly browned. Watch carefully.

Makes 8 servings.

Fit For a King

rasshopper Pie

20 cream-filled chocolate cookies
1 14-ounce can sweetened
condensed milk
3 tablespoons green crème de
menthe

2 tablespoons white crème de cacao
1 cup heavy cream, whipped
Mint for garnish

■ In a bowl crush 20 cream-filled chocolate cookies to make 1¾ cups of crumbs. Reserve ¼ cup for garnish. Pat the remaining crumbs on the bottom and sides of a buttered 9-inch pie tin. Set the crust aside.

In a medium bowl combine the condensed milk, crème de menthe, crème de cacao, and heavy cream. Mix thoroughly. Pour the mixture into the crust. Top with the remaining crumbs. Freeze the pie for 6 hours. The pie will not freeze solid. Garnish with mint.

Makes 8 servings.

☆ **GETTING a little coaching as he goes over his lines**

$\mathcal{F}$ruit Sundae Pie

1 9-inch pie crust, baked
1 cup heavy cream
1 quart vanilla ice cream

1 quart fresh strawberries
½ cup walnuts, chopped

■ Let the pie shell cool thoroughly. In a mixing bowl beat the cream until thick. Fill the pie shell with the vanilla ice cream. Arrange the strawberries over the ice cream. Frost with the whipped cream and sprinkle with nuts. Serve immediately.

Makes 8 servings.

$\mathcal{C}$herry Pie

Pastry for 1 8-inch 2-crust pie
½ cup sugar
Salt to taste

3 tablespoons all-purpose flour
2½ cups canned sour red cherries
4 drops almond extract

■ Line a pie pan with 1 layer of crust. In a saucepan mix together the sugar, salt, and flour. Drain the juice from the cherries, reserving ¾ cup of juice. Add the cherry juice to the saucepan. Cook over direct heat, stirring constantly, until the mixture boils and thickens. Remove the pan from the heat. Add the almond extract. Place the cherries in the pie crust. Pour in the thickened juice.

Roll out the second pastry for the upper crust. Cut out vents for steam. Moisten the edges of the lower crust with water. Place the top crust over the cherry filling. Press the edges together and trim off any excess dough. Let the pie stand for 10 minutes. Flute the edges.

Bake at 450° for 15 minutes or until the crust is light browned. Reduce the heat to 325° and continue baking about 15 minutes more. Let the pie cool before serving.

Makes 6 servings.

Fit For a King

lueberry Pie

Pastry for 1 8-inch 2-crust pie
1 quart fresh blueberries, washed
1½ tablespoons fresh lemon juice
1 tablespoon grated lemon rind

¾ cup sugar
¼ teaspoon salt
2 tablespoons all-purpose flour

■ In a mixing bowl combine the blueberries, lemon juice, and lemon rind. Toss in the sugar, salt, and flour. Line a pie pan with 1 layer of crust.

Turn the blueberry mixture into the pie shell. Moisten the rim of the bottom crust. Place the top crust over the filling and pinch the edges to seal. Make air vents in the top crust to allow steam to escape. Bake at 450° for about 10 minutes. Reduce the heat to 350° and bake about 30 minutes more. Let the pie cool before serving.

Makes 6 servings.

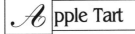pple Tart

1⅔ cups all-purpose flour
½ teaspoon salt
½ cup butter
2 tablespoons water

4 large apples, peeled, cored, and
sliced
4 teaspoons sugar

■ Into a mixing bowl sift together the flour and salt. Cut in the butter until the mixture resembles bread crumbs. Make a well in the center and pour the water into the well. Mix until a dough forms. Divide the dough in half and roll out half on a floured board. Place the dough in a pie plate. Arrange the apples over the bottom crust. Sprinkle with sugar. Roll out the remaining dough and place it over the apples. Pinch the edges closed. Prick the dough with a fork 5 or 6 times, and make a small hole in the center. Bake at 425° for 30 minutes or until brown.

Makes 8 servings.

☆ ELVIS, with his hands full, enjoys a kiss from
Dolores Hart and Jan Shepard.

$\mathscr{A}$ pricot Pie

2 cups canned apricots, drained
   and juice reserved
¼ cup sugar
1½ cups apricot juice
1 3-ounce package lemon gelatin

½ cup water
Salt to taste
1 8-inch pie crust, baked
½ cup heavy cream, whipped

■ In a mixing bowl combine the apricots and sugar, and refrigerate until chilled. In a saucepan bring the apricot juice to a boil. Remove the pan from the heat and add the gelatin. Add the water and salt. Refrigerate the mixture until it begins to thicken.

Arrange the apricots in the pie shell. Spoon the thickened gelatin mixture over the apricots. Refrigerate the pie until the gelatin congeals. Top with whipped cream.

Makes 6 servings.

Fit For a King

Sweet Potato Pie

2 medium sweet potatoes
1½ cups butter
2 cups sugar
4 eggs
1 tablespoon cornstarch

¼ cup evaporated milk
2 teaspoons vanilla extract
Dash lemon flavoring
2 9-inch pie crusts

■ Boil the sweet potatoes until tender. In a mixing bowl mash them with the butter, blending well. Add the sugar and beat until smooth. Blend in the eggs, cornstarch, milk, vanilla, and lemon flavoring, beating well. Pour the filling into the pie shells. Bake at 350° for 1 hour or until done.

Makes 12 to 16 servings.

Peach Cobbler

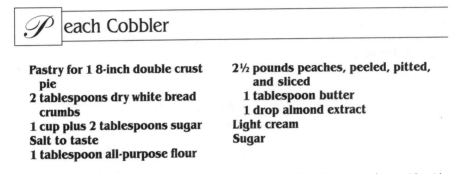

Pastry for 1 8-inch double crust pie
2 tablespoons dry white bread crumbs
1 cup plus 2 tablespoons sugar
Salt to taste
1 tablespoon all-purpose flour

2½ pounds peaches, peeled, pitted, and sliced
1 tablespoon butter
1 drop almond extract
Light cream
Sugar

■ Place the oven rack in the center of the oven. Roll out ¾ of the pastry into a 10 x 14-inch rectangle. Fold the pastry in half and gently place it in a 6 x 10-inch baking pan. The pastry will extend over the edges of the pan. Sprinkle the bread crumbs in the bottom of the pastry.

In a medium bowl combine the sugar, salt, and flour. Sprinkle ¼ cup of the sugar mixture over the bread crumbs. Arrange the peach slices in the pastry, and dot them with butter. Add the almond extract. Sprinkle the remaining sugar mixture over the peaches. Fold the extended dough over the peaches, tucking in the corners. The center will not be covered with pastry.

Roll out the remaining pastry into a 3 x 7-inch rectangle. Cut a line down the center for ventilation. Place the pastry over the peaches. Brush the entire top with cream and sprinkle with sugar. Bake at 450° for 15 minutes or until the crust begins to brown. Reduce the heat to 325° and bake for 25 minutes more. Remove the cobbler to a rack to cool. Serve with the remaining cream.

Makes 6 servings.

Desserts

$\mathscr{B}$ anana Cream Pie

⅓ cup all-purpose flour
½ cup sugar
¼ teaspoon salt
2 cups milk, scalded
2 eggs, separated

½ teaspoon vanilla extract
3 ripe bananas, peeled and sliced
1 8-inch pie crust, baked
¼ cup sugar

■ In the top of a double boiler blend the flour, ½ cup sugar and salt. Slowly add 1 cup of the hot milk and blend until smooth. Add the remaining milk. Cook over direct heat, stirring constantly, until the mixture begins to boil and becomes thick.

In a separate bowl beat the egg yolks with a little of the hot milk mixture. Return the egg mixture to the top of the double boiler. Place the pan over boiling water and cook for about 2 minutes, stirring constantly. Remove the pan from the water and add the vanilla. Place the banana slices in the bottom of the pie shell. Pour in the hot mixture. Let the pie cool.

In a bowl beat the egg whites until foamy. Beat in ¼ cup of sugar until smooth. Pile the meringue on top of the filling. Place the pie on a baking sheet. Bake at 350° for 15 minutes or until golden brown. Let the pie cool before serving.

Makes 6 servings.

$\mathscr{W}$HILE he was in the army, Elvis's mail averaged 15,000 letters a week. He also received packages of cakes, pies, and cookies, which he shared with his fellow G.I.'s.

Mississippi Mud Pie

1 cup all-purpose flour
¼ cup butter
½ cup chopped walnuts
1 cup confectioners' sugar
1 8-ounce package cream cheese,
  softened

1 cup cream, whipped
1 6-ounce package instant chocolate
  pudding mix
4 cups milk
Whipped topping
Chopped nuts for garnish

■ In a mixing bowl combine the flour, butter, and walnuts. Press the mixture into a 9 x 13-inch pan. Bake at 350° for 12 minutes. Let the layer cool.

In a separate bowl combine the confectioners' sugar, cream cheese, and cream. Spread the mixture over the first layer. In a large bowl prepare the pudding mix with the milk according to the package directions. Spread the pudding over the second layer. Cover with whipped topping and sprinkle with nuts. Refrigerate for 4 hours.

Makes 8 servings.

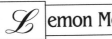
Lemon Meringue Pie

1½ cups sugar
⅓ cup cornstarch
1½ cups water
3 eggs, separated
3 tablespoons butter

¼ cup fresh lemon juice
1⅓ tablespoons grated lemon rind
¼ teaspoon cream of tartar
6 tablespoons sugar
1 9-inch pie crust, baked

■ In a saucepan combine the sugar and cornstarch. Add the water and cook over medium heat, stirring constantly until thickened. Bring the mixture to a boil, and boil for 1 minute. Remove the pan from the heat. In a medium bowl beat the egg yolks lightly. Pour a small amount of the hot liquid into the egg yolks, stirring constantly. Return the yolk mixture to the saucepan, stirring constantly. Bring the mixture to a boil, and boil until thickened. Blend in the butter, lemon juice, and lemon rind. Pour the filling into the pie shell.

In a large bowl beat the egg whites with the cream of tartar and 6 tablespoons of sugar until stiff. Spread the meringue over the pie filling, making sure the meringue touches the edges of the pie. Bake at 400° for 8 minutes, or until the meringue is light brown. Let the pie cool before serving.

Makes 8 servings.

Desserts

$\mathcal{S}$ weet Chocolate Pie

2 egg whites, room temperature
Dash salt
Dash cream of tartar

½ cup sugar
½ cup finely chopped walnuts
½ teaspoon vanilla extract

Filling
1 4-ounce package sweet chocolate
3 tablespoons water
1 teaspoon vanilla extract

1 tablespoon brandy
1 cup heavy cream

■ In a mixing bowl combine the egg whites, salt, and cream of tartar. Beat until foamy. Add the sugar, 2 tablespoons at a time, beating until stiff after each addition. Fold in the nuts and vanilla. Spoon the mixture into a lightly greased 8-inch pie pan, spreading to form a pie shell and extending the sides ½ inch over the edge of the pan. Bake at 300° for 55 minutes. Let the shell cool.

In a saucepan combine the chocolate and water, and cook over low heat until the chocolate has melted. Let the chocolate cool. Add the vanilla and brandy. In a bowl whip the cream to a soft consistency. Fold the cream into the chocolate. Pour the filling into the pie shell. Refrigerate the pie for 2 hours before serving.

Makes 6 servings.

$\mathcal{P}$ eanut Butter Pie

1 9-inch pie crust, unbaked
1 cup peanut butter
1 teaspoon vanilla extract
1½ cups sugar

½ teaspoon salt
2 eggs, well beaten
1½ cups milk

■ In a mixing bowl cream together the peanut butter and vanilla. Gradually add the sugar and salt, blending well. Add the eggs and milk. Blend thoroughly.

Turn the filling into the pie crust. Bake at 450° for 10 minutes. Reduce the heat to 350° and bake for 25 minutes or until a knife inserted in the center comes out clean. Let the pie cool on a wire rack.

Makes 6 servings.

Fit For a King

☆ **WITH Ursula Andress in *Fun in Acapulco***

*E*LVIS *liked to greet each of his leading ladies
in a unique way. His calling card was to send each a big bouquet of
flowers when she arrived at the studio. This was followed by a box of
chocolates and another bouquet of flowers—this one red carnations
—with his card attached.*

$\mathscr{L}$ emon Chiffon Pie

2 teaspoons gelatin	1 tablespoon butter, melted
⅓ cup cold water	½ teaspoon grated lemon rind
4 egg yolks	4 egg whites
¾ cup sugar	½ cup sugar
⅛ teaspoon salt	1 9-inch pie crust, baked
½ cup fresh lemon juice	

Topping
½ cup cream ½ cup grated coconut
1 teaspoon sugar

■ In a measuring cup soften the gelatin in 2 tablespoons of cold water. In a mixing bowl beat the egg yolks until thick. Add ¾ cup of sugar, the salt, lemon juice, and remaining water. Mix well. Pour the mixture into the top of a double boiler. Place the pan over simmering water and cook until the mixture is thickened, about 5 minutes. Add the butter during the last minute of cooking. Remove the pan from the water. Add the gelatin and lemon rind, stirring to dissolve the gelatin. Set the pan in a larger pan of ice water until the mixture begins to thicken, stirring occasionally.

In a large bowl beat the egg whites with a dash of salt until stiff. Add ½ cup of sugar and beat until stiff. With a rubber spatula fold the egg whites carefully but thoroughly into the lemon mixture. Pour the filling into the baked pie crust, spreading evenly. Refrigerate for 3 hours or until set.

In a mixing bowl beat the cream until thick. Blend in the sugar. Spread the whipped cream over the pie and top with coconut.

Makes 6 servings.

$\mathscr{P}$ eanut Butter Squares

1 cup finely crushed graham crackers	1 cup creamy peanut butter
2 cups confectioners' sugar	1 12-ounce package chocolate chips, melted
½ cup butter	

■ In a bowl combine the graham crackers and confectioners' sugar. Cream the butter and peanut butter, and add the graham cracker mixture. Spread into an ungreased 9-inch square pan. Drizzle the melted chocolate over the top. Refrigerate for 3 hours.

Makes 12 servings.

Fit For a King

194

$\mathcal{G}$ ingersnaps

2 eggs	**1 teaspoon baking soda**
1 cup molasses	**¾ teaspoon ginger**
⅔ cup butter	**1 teaspoon cloves**
1 cup sugar	**3½ cups all-purpose flour**

■ In a mixing bowl beat the eggs. Add the molasses, butter, and sugar. Into a separate bowl sift together the dry ingredients. Fold the sifted mixture into the molasses batter. Blend well. Roll the dough into small balls and place them on a greased baking sheet about 2 inches apart. Bake at 350° for 15 minutes.

Makes 6 dozen.

☆ **WITH Stella Stevens in** *Girls! Girls! Girls!*

☆ **WITH Mary Tyler Moore in** *A Change of Habit*

$\mathscr{C}$ ounty Fair Cookies

5 cups oatmeal	1 teaspoon salt
2 cups butter	2 teaspoons baking powder
2 cups sugar	2 teaspoons baking soda
2 cups packed light brown sugar	1 24-ounce package semisweet
4 eggs	chocolate chips
2 teaspoons vanilla extract	1 8-ounce milk chocolate bar, grated
4 cups all-purpose flour	3 cups walnuts, chopped

■ Place the oatmeal in a blender or food processor. Process until the oats turn powdery. In a mixing bowl cream together the butter, sugar, and brown sugar. Add the eggs and vanilla.

In a separate bowl combine the flour and processed oatmeal. Blend in the salt, baking powder, and baking soda. Fold the dry ingredients into the creamed mixture. Add the chocolate chips, grated chocolate bar, and walnuts.

Shape the dough into small balls and place them on a greased baking sheet about 2 inches apart. Bake at 350° for 10 minutes. Do not overbake.

Makes 5 dozen.

Fit For a King

*C*hocolate-dipped Macaroons

4 large egg whites
1½ teaspoons vanilla extract
⅔ cup sugar
¼ cup all-purpose flour

3½ cups sweetened flaked coconut
¼ cup butter
1 8-ounce package of semisweet
    chocolate chips, chopped

■ In a large bowl beat the egg whites until frothy. Add the vanilla, sugar, and flour. Mix until smooth. Stir in the coconut until evenly moistened. Using a ¼ cup measure, spoon the mixture onto 2 greased 12 x 15-inch baking sheets making 10 mounds. Pat each flat. Bake at 325° for about 25 minutes or until the macaroons are golden brown. Transfer the macaroons to cooling racks.

In the top of a double boiler over simmering water melt the butter and chocolate, stirring occasionally. Remove the pans from the heat, keeping the chocolate mixture over the water.

Dip half of each macaroon into the chocolate, tipping the pan and scraping the sides to collect chocolate. Line a baking sheet with waxed paper. Set the macaroons apart. Refrigerate uncovered for 45 minutes or until the chocolate hardens.

Makes 10.

☆ WITH Barbara Stanwyck in *Roustabout*

Desserts

$\mathcal{P}$eanut Butter Brownies

¾ cup creamy peanut butter
⅓ cup butter
2 cups sugar
1 cup packed light brown sugar
4 eggs

1½ teaspoons vanilla extract
3 cups all-purpose flour
1 tablespoon baking powder
½ teaspoon salt
¼ cup chopped peanuts

Topping
1½ cups packed light brown sugar
½ cup butter
¼ cup milk

1 tablespoon honey
1 cup chopped peanuts

■ In a mixing bowl cream the peanut butter, ⅓ cup of butter, sugar, and 1 cup of brown sugar. Add the eggs and vanilla, and beat until well blended. Into a separate bowl sift the flour, baking powder, and salt. Fold the dry ingredients into the creamed mixture with ¼ cup of chopped peanuts and beat until smooth. Spread the batter into a 9 x 13-inch baking pan. Bake at 350° for 35 minutes.

In a saucepan combine 1½ cups of brown sugar, ½ cup of butter, milk, and honey. Bring the mixture to a boil, and cook it slowly for 10 minutes. Remove the topping from the heat and add 1 cup of peanuts. Let the topping cool and spread it over the warm brownies.

Makes 12.

$\mathcal{E}$LVIS *was seen at Graceland making peach ice cream to go with a freshly baked cake. The family was sitting around waiting for him to finish so they could have their ice cream and cake.*

ocha Pecan Bars

¼ cup chocolate fudge sauce
1 18-ounce box yellow cake mix
1 3-ounce package instant vanilla
   pudding
1 egg
1½ cups sherry
¼ cup instant coffee

2 teaspoons vanilla extract
1 teaspoon almond extract
¼ cup oil
¼ cup warm honey
1 cup raisins
1 cup whole pecans

■ In a saucepan melt the fudge sauce. Set it aside. In a large mixing bowl combine the cake mix, pudding mix, egg, 1 cup of sherry, coffee, vanilla, almond extract, and oil. Beat the batter slowly. Add the honey and blend well. Add the remaining sherry. Fold in the raisins and pecans. Spread the batter into a greased and floured 9 x 13-inch pan. Drizzle the fudge sauce over the batter. Bake at 350° for 35 minutes. Let the bars cool before serving.

Makes 12.

☆ ELVIS is greeted in Hawaii where he gave a benefit concert for the
Arizona Battleship Memorial in 1960.

Desserts

☆ **SHOWING** off his talents on the drums

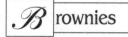 rownies

1 14-ounce package caramels	1 egg
⅔ cup evaporated milk	1 cup chopped walnuts
1 cup butter	1 12-ounce package semisweet
1 18-ounce package German	chocolate chips
chocolate cake mix	1 16-ounce can chocolate frosting

■ In the top of a double boiler over simmering water combine the caramels, ⅓ cup of evaporated milk, and ¼ cup of butter. Stir frequently until melted and smooth.

Melt the remaining ¾ cup of butter. In a large mixing bowl combine the cake mix, melted butter, egg, ⅓ cup of evaporated milk, and nuts. Press half of the cake mixture into the bottom of a 9 x 13-inch baking pan. Sprinkle the chocolate chips over the dough. Pour the melted caramels over the chocolate. Top with the remaining dough. Bake at 350° for 20 minutes. Frost with the chocolate frosting. Let the brownies cool before serving.

Makes 12.

Fit For a King

Fudge Cookies

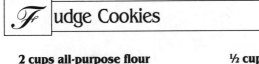

2 cups all-purpose flour	½ cup packed light brown sugar
1½ teaspoons baking powder	2 eggs, beaten
¼ teaspoon salt	1 teaspoon vanilla extract
½ teaspoon baking soda	2 1-ounce squares unsweetened
½ cup butter	chocolate, melted
½ cup sugar	¼ cup buttermilk

■ Into a mixing bowl sift the flour. Measure 2 cups and resift 3 times with the baking powder, salt, and baking soda. In a separate bowl cream the butter. Add the sugar and brown sugar, and beat until smooth. Add the eggs and beat until fluffy. Add the vanilla. Stir in the cooled melted chocolate. Add the flour mixture in three separate portions, alternating with the buttermilk. Begin and end with the flour.

Drop by heaping teaspoonfuls onto a greased baking sheet about 2 inches apart. Bake at 375° for 12 minutes. Remove the cookies and place them on a rack to cool.

Makes 4 dozen.

Sugar Cookies

5 cups all-purpose flour	2 eggs
1 teaspoon baking soda	2 teaspoons vanilla extract
2 cups sugar	1 teaspoon cream of tartar
1 cup butter	Pinch salt
1 cup oil	

■ Into a mixing bowl sift the flour and baking soda. Add the remaining ingredients. Refrigerate the dough for 3 hours. Shape into balls and place them on an ungreased baking sheet. Flatten with a fork and sprinkle with sugar. Bake at 375° for about 8 minutes.

Makes 6 dozen.

Desserts

☆ **ELVIS in the army**

*F*ANS *constantly asked Elvis if he had
received the cookies or cakes they had sent him while he was stationed
in Germany. Knowing that each treat was prepared out of the kindness
of their hearts, Elvis always responded as if he had
personally received the package.
On average, he received 800 packages of tempting desserts weekly.
Elvis thanked his fans, telling them that he shared the packages with his
buddies. He added that they were the best fed unit in the entire outfit.*

$\mathcal{G}$erman Chocolate Oatmeal Cookies

1 cup plus 2 tablespoons butter
2 cups packed light brown sugar
2 eggs
3 cups quick cooking oats
2½ cups all-purpose flour
2 teaspoons vanilla extract
1 teaspoon baking soda

1 teaspoon salt
2 cups chopped pecans
1 14-ounce can sweetened
   condensed milk
1 12-ounce package semisweet
   chocolate chips
½ cup shredded coconut

■ In a large mixing bowl cream the butter and 1 cup of brown sugar. Add the eggs one at a time, beating well after each addition. Add the oats, flour, 1 teaspoon of vanilla, baking soda, and salt. Mix in 1 cup of the pecans. Set the mixture aside.

In the top of a double boiler over simmering water combine the milk and chocolate, stirring constantly until the chocolate melts. Add the remaining pecans, coconut, 2 tablespoons of butter, and 1 teaspoon of vanilla. Blend well. Spread ⅔ of the oat mixture into a 10 x 15-inch baking pan. Spread the chocolate mixture over the first layer. Crumble the remaining oat mixture over the chocolate layer. Bake at 350° for 25 minutes. Let the cookies cool before cutting.

Makes 5 dozen.

$\mathcal{A}$lmond Spice Cookies

1 cup butter
½ cup packed light brown sugar
2¼ cups all-purpose flour
1 teaspoon ginger
½ teaspoon cinnamon

½ teaspoon salt
1 egg
½ teaspoon vanilla extract
1 7½-ounce package almonds

■ In a large bowl cream the butter with the brown sugar. Add the remaining ingredients except the almonds. Drop the mixture by teaspoonfuls onto an ungreased baking sheet. Press an almond into the center of each cookie. Bake at 400° for about 10 minutes or until set but not brown.

Makes 6 dozen.

raline Cookies

½ cup butter
1½ cups packed light brown sugar
1 egg

1 teaspoon vanilla extract
1½ cups all-purpose flour
1 cup chopped pecans

■ In a bowl cream the butter. Add the brown sugar and egg and beat until smooth. Add the vanilla. Sift in the flour, and mix well. Add the nuts and blend thoroughly. Shape the dough into small balls and place on a cookie sheet 1 inch apart. Flatten with a fork. Bake at 375° for about 12 minutes. Let the cookies cool before serving.

Makes 3 servings.

offee

1 cup butter
1 cup sugar
3 tablespoons water

1 teaspoon vanilla extract
½ pound milk chocolate
1½ cups pecans

■ Butter an 8-inch square pan. In a saucepan melt the butter. Add the sugar and water, blending constantly. Cook until the mixtures reaches 300° on a candy thermometer. Blend in the vanilla. Quickly pour the candy mixture into the prepared pan, spreading the mixture evenly into the corners. Mark into squares with a sharp knife. Set it aside to cool.

In the top of a double boiler over simmering water melt the chocolate. Remove the pan from the hot water and stir the chocolate until smooth. Set it aside to cool.

When the candy has cooled, spread half of the chocolate over the top. Sprinkle with half of the pecans. Invert the candy onto waxed paper and pour the remaining chocolate over it. Sprinkle with the remaining pecans. Cool.

Makes 1 pound.

Taffy

2 cups sugar	**1 tablespoon butter**
1¼ cups white corn syrup	**1¼ teaspoons salt**
1 cup water	**Peppermint extract**

■ Butter a large shallow pan and set aside. In a saucepan combine the sugar, corn syrup, and water. Stir over low heat until the sugar is dissolved. Increase the heat and bring the mixture to boiling. Cook, stirring constantly until the mixture reaches 244° on a candy thermometer. Remove the saucepan from the heat.

Blend in the butter and salt. Pour the mixture into the bottom of the prepared pan. Do not scrape the bottom or sides of the saucepan. Let the mixture cool enough to handle.

Pull portions of the taffy with lightly greased fingers. Work with the candy until it is cool and no longer sticky. While pulling add peppermint extract to taste. Place on waxed paper. Cut each portion into 1-inch pieces.

Makes 6 dozen.

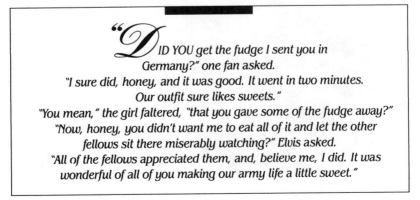

"*D*ID YOU get the fudge I sent you in
Germany?" one fan asked.
"I sure did, honey, and it was good. It went in two minutes.
Our outfit sure likes sweets."
"You mean," the girl faltered, "that you gave some of the fudge away?"
"Now, honey, you didn't want me to eat all of it and let the other
fellows sit there miserably watching?" Elvis asked.
"All of the fellows appreciated them, and, believe me, I did. It was
wonderful of all of you making our army life a little sweet."

hocolate Mint Truffles

1 cup semisweet chocolate chips
2 tablespoons unsalted butter
¼ cup heavy cream

¼ cup peppermint Schnapps
¼ cup unsweetened cocoa powder
3 tablespoons confectioners' sugar

■ In a saucepan melt the chocolate chips with the butter. Add the heavy cream and peppermint Schnapps. Gently stir over moderate heat until smooth. Pour the mixture into a small bowl. Cover and refrigerate until firm.

Into a separate bowl sift together the cocoa powder and sugar. Place the bowl with the truffle mixture into a pan of ice water. Shape the mixture into 1-inch balls. Roll each ball in the cocoa mixture until thoroughly coated. Refrigerate the truffles before serving.

Makes 8.

☆ **WITH one of his favorite entertainers, Jackie Wilson**

Fudge

**3 6-ounce packages semisweet
chocolate chips**
**1 14-ounce can sweetened
condensed milk**

1½ cups chopped walnuts
1½ teaspoons vanilla extract

■ Line an 8-inch square baking pan with waxed paper. In a heavy saucepan combine the chocolate chips and condensed milk. Cook over low heat, stirring constantly, until the chocolate melts. Remove the pan from the heat and stir in the nuts and vanilla. Spread the mixture evenly in the prepared pan. Refrigerate the fudge until firm. Cut into squares.

Makes 36 pieces.

Chocolate Caramel Apples

1 cup packed light brown sugar
¼ cup white corn syrup
¼ cup milk
**1 1-ounce square unsweetened
chocolate**

3 tablespoons butter
4 apples, washed
4 wooden sticks

■ In the top of a double boiler combine the brown sugar, syrup, milk, and chocolate. Place the pan over direct heat and cook until a drop in cold water forms a hard ball. Stir to prevent sticking. Add the butter and cook for 3 minutes. Place the pan over simmering water to keep warm and smooth while dipping the apples.

Push a wooden stick through the core of the apple at the stem end. Hold the stick and dip the apple in the syrup. Twirl the apple to coat evenly. Stand each apple upright on waxed paper. Let the apples cool.

Makes 4 servings.

$\mathscr{B}$ anana Split Torte

12 graham crackers
1 cup sugar
¼ cup butter, melted
1 cup finely chopped dry roasted
  peanuts
2 eggs
1 cup butter

2 cups confectioners' sugar
4 large bananas
1 pint strawberries
1 20-ounce can crushed pineapple,
  drained
1 cup whipping cream, whipped

■ In a bowl crush the graham crackers. Add the sugar and melted butter. Blend in the roasted peanuts. Set aside ¼ cup for the topping. Press the remaining mixture into the bottom of a 9 x 13-inch pan.

In a separate bowl beat the eggs with the butter and confectioners' sugar. Beat about 15 minutes. Spread the mixture over the crumb mixture. Add the sliced bananas. Top with the strawberries and crushed pineapple. Spread the whipped cream over the fruit. Top with the remaining crumb mixture. Refrigerate 4 to 6 hours.

Makes 8 servings.

$\mathscr{C}$ herry Delight

6 egg whites
1 teaspoon cream of tartar
2 cups sugar
2 cups coarsely broken salted
  crackers

1 cup chopped walnuts
1 cup whipping cream
1 21-ounce can cherry pie filling

■ In a bowl beat the egg whites and cream of tartar until foamy. Continue beating while slowly adding the sugar to make a meringue. Add the crackers and mix just to blend. Spread the meringue into a 9 x 13-inch cake pan. Sprinkle with nuts. Bake at 350° for 35 minutes. Let it cool. Cover the meringue with whipping cream and pie filling.

Makes 8 servings.

 hubarb-Strawberry Crisp

½ cup sugar
3 tablespoons cornstarch
3 cups fresh rhubarb slices
2 cups sliced fresh strawberries
1¼ cups quick oats

½ cup packed light brown sugar
½ cup butter, melted
½ cup all-purpose flour
1 teaspoon cinnamon

■ In a large bowl combine the sugar and cornstarch. Add the rhubarb and strawberries, tossing to coat. Spoon the fruit into an 8-inch square baking dish.

In a separate bowl combine the oats, brown sugar, butter, flour, and cinnamon, blending until the mixture resembles coarse crumbs. Sprinkle the topping over the fruit. Bake at 350° for 30 minutes. Let the crisp cool before serving.

Makes 8 servings.

 utch Apple Crisp

½ cup sugar
3 tablespoons all-purpose flour
½ teaspoon cinnamon
¼ cup packed light brown sugar
⅛ teaspoon salt

¼ teaspoon nutmeg
5½ cups cooking apples, peeled, cored, and sliced
1 tablespoon fresh lemon juice

Topping
¾ cup all-purpose flour
⅓ cup butter, at room temperature

¼ cup sugar
¼ cup packed light brown sugar

■ In a mixing bowl combine ½ cup of sugar, 3 tablespoons of flour, cinnamon, ¼ cup of brown sugar, salt, and nutmeg. Add the apples and lemon juice, tossing well. Spoon the mixture into a greased casserole dish.

In a separate bowl combine ¾ cup of flour, the butter, ¼ cup of sugar, and ¼ cup of brown sugar. Blend the mixture with a fork until crumbly. Sprinkle the topping over the apples. Bake at 375° for 50 minutes or until the top is golden and the filling is bubbling. Let the crisp cool before serving.

Makes 8 servings.

$\mathscr{D}$ oughnuts

3 tablespoons shortening	4 teaspoons baking powder
⅔ cup sugar	½ teaspoon salt
2 eggs, well beaten	⅔ cup milk
3½ cups sifted all-purpose flour	Confectioners' sugar

■ In a mixing bowl cream the shortening with the sugar. Add the eggs and blend. In a separate bowl sift together the dry ingredients and add them to the creamed mixture alternately with the milk. Turn the dough onto a floured board and roll to 1-inch thickness. Cut with floured doughnut cutter.

Fry the doughnuts a few at a time in deep hot fat (365°). Turn just as soon as the doughnuts rise to the top. Turn once or twice during the frying process. Drain on paper towels. Let the doughnuts cool. Dust with confectioners' sugar.

Makes 18.

$\mathscr{C}$ hocolate Mousse

1 12-ounce package semisweet chocolate chips	1 tablespoon instant coffee
6 eggs, separated	2 cups heavy cream

■ In the top of a double boiler over simmering water melt the chocolate chips. Remove the pan from the water. Slowly stir the egg yolks into the cooling chocolate. In a measuring cup add just enough water to the coffee to create a paste. Add the coffee to the chocolate.

In a large bowl beat the egg whites until stiff. Fold the egg whites into the chocolate. In a small bowl beat the cream until thick. Fold the cream into the chocolate. Pour the mousse into a 9 x 13-inch pan and refrigerate it for 1 hour before serving.

Makes 6 servings.

aple Mousse

1 cup maple syrup
4 egg yolks

Salt to taste
2 cups evaporated milk

■ In a saucepan boil the syrup. In a mixing bowl beat the egg yolks until thick and add the salt. Remove the syrup and pour it slowly over the egg yolks, stirring constantly. Let the mixture cool. Whip the evaporated milk and fold it into the syrup. Pour the mousse into a mold and refrigerate for 4 hours.

Makes 4 servings.

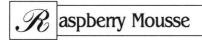

LVIS insisted that he didn't go to parties.
"I don't like parties. I like to give my own. I don't like a lot of noise, and I don't drink or smoke. I would rather sit around and talk and play records, have a Coke and something to eat. If it were possible, I'd let anyone in who came to see me."

aspberry Mousse

1½ cups raspberry juice
Juice from ½ lemon

20 marshmallows
1½ cups cream

■ In a saucepan heat the juice. Strain. Cut the marshmallows into pieces and dissolve them in the juice. Add the lemon juice. In a bowl beat the cream until stiff. Blend the whipped cream into the juice and mix until smooth and creamy. Fill 2 sherbet glasses with the mousse. Refrigerate until chilled.

Makes 2 servings.

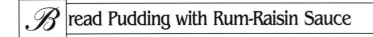# $\mathscr{B}$read Pudding with Rum-Raisin Sauce

10 slices day-old bread	1 teaspoon vanilla extract
4 cups milk, heated	¼ teaspoon nutmeg
1 cup light cream	1 teaspoon cinnamon
4 eggs	¼ cup butter, melted
1 cup sugar	½ cup raisins

Rum Raisin Sauce

3 egg yolks	½ cup raisins
1 cup sugar	1 tablespoon cornstarch
1 teaspoon vanilla extract	¼ cup hot water
1½ cups milk	3 tablespoons rum

■ In a large bowl combine the bread, 4 cups of milk, and the cream. In a medium bowl beat the eggs lightly. Add 1 cup of sugar and the bread mixture. Stir in 1 teaspoon of vanilla, the nutmeg, cinnamon, butter, and ½ cup of raisins. Pour the mixture into a buttered 2-quart baking dish. Set the dish in a larger shallow pan. Add water in the larger pan to a depth of 1 inch. Bake at 350° for 1 hour or until a knife inserted in the center comes out clean.

In a small saucepan beat the egg yolks lightly and add 1 cup of sugar, 1 teaspoon of vanilla, 1½ cups of milk, and ½ cup of raisins. Blend well. Cook over low heat, stirring constantly, until the mixture boils. In a small bowl blend the cornstarch and water until smooth. Stir the mixture into the saucepan. Return to a boil, stirring constantly. Add the rum. Serve the sauce over the pudding.

Makes 6 servings.

$\mathscr{C}$ream Puffs

1 cup boiling water	1 cup pastry flour, sifted
½ cup butter	3 eggs

■ In a saucepan of boiling water add the butter and salt. Blend in the flour, stirring constantly, until the mixture leaves the sides of the pan. Add the eggs one at a time, until each egg is thoroughly blended.

Drop by tablespoonfuls onto a greased baking sheet. Bake at 400° for about 30 minutes. Cream puffs may be filled with vanilla ice cream and topped with chocolate syrup.

Makes 1 dozen.

Fit For a King

ℬ anana Pudding

1 tablespoon gelatin
¼ cup cold water
1 cup boiling water
1 cup sugar

¼ cup fresh lemon juice
3 egg whites, stiffly beaten
3 bananas, peeled and sliced

■ In a bowl soften the gelatin in the cold water for 5 minutes. Then add the boiling water and stir to dissolve. Blend in the sugar and lemon juice, and strain. Refrigerate the mixture until somewhat thickened. Whip until frothy. Fold in the beaten egg whites.

Dip a mold into cold water. Arrange the sliced bananas in the mold. Pour in the gelatin mixture. Refrigerate until firm. Unmold and serve.

Makes 4 servings.

𝒫 ound Cake Pudding

1 pound cake, cut into ½-inch
    cubes
2 tablespoons golden raisins
1 cup milk
½ cup fresh orange juice

2 eggs
2 teaspoons sugar
½ teaspoon grated orange rind
2 teaspoons confectioners' sugar

■ Grease two 10-ounce custard cups with butter. Fill each with cake cubes and 1 tablespoon of raisins. Set the cups aside.

In a mixing bowl whisk together the milk, orange juice, eggs, sugar, and orange rind. Pour half of this mixture into each custard cup. Place the cups in an 8-inch square pan filled with water to the depth of about 1 inch.

Bake at 350° for 40 minutes or until a toothpick inserted in the center comes out clean. Remove the baking pan from the oven and the cups from the water. Place the cups on a wire rack to cool. Before serving sift half the confectioners' sugar over each cake.

Makes 2 servings.

Desserts

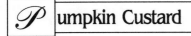umpkin Custard

1 cup canned pumpkin	Dash ginger
2 eggs, slightly beaten	½ teaspoon cinnamon
½ cup packed light brown sugar	1 cup cream
¼ teaspoon salt	⅛ teaspoon grated orange rind

■ In a mixing bowl combine the pumpkin with the eggs, brown sugar, salt, ginger, and cinnamon. Blend in the cream and orange rind. Pour the mixture into 4 custard cups.

Set the cups in a large pan of hot water. The water should almost reach the top of the custard cups. Bake at 325° for 40 minutes.

Makes 4 servings.

On NOVEMBER 6, 1954, Elvis signed a contract with the "Louisiana Hayride" that called for him to appear on the show for fifty-two consecutive Saturday nights between 8:00 and 11:00 P.M. As a part of his duties as a regular performer, he sang a short commercial ditty for Southern Doughnuts that described them as "Pipin' Hot."

Maple Custard

2 large eggs	2 cups milk, scalded
⅓ cup sugar	Dash nutmeg
¼ teaspoon salt	2 tablespoons maple syrup

■ In a mixing bowl beat the eggs with the sugar and salt. Pour in the hot milk. Place 1 teaspoon of maple syrup in each of 6 custard cups. Strain the egg mixture into the cups. Sprinkle with nutmeg. Place the custard cups in a baking pan and fill the pan with enough water to come halfway up the sides of the custard cups. Bake at 350° for about 35 minutes or until a knife inserted through the custard comes out clean. Cool and serve.

Makes 6.

☆ IN THE STUDIO recording "Hound Dog"

$\mathcal{P}$ each Ice Cream

1½ cups peaches, peeled, pitted, and mashed	Salt to taste
	1 tablespoon all-purpose flour
1¼ cups sugar	1 cup cream
1 cup milk	1 tablespoon vanilla extract

■ In a mixing bowl blend the peaches with ¾ cup of sugar, and set the mixture aside. In a saucepan scald the milk. In a separate bowl combine ½ cup of sugar, the salt, and flour. Gradually add the mixture to the milk and cook over low heat, stirring constantly. Bring the mixture to a boil, and boil for 1 minute. Add the mashed peaches. Pour the mixture into a freezer can and freeze for about 30 minutes.

In a mixing bowl whip the cream until somewhat stiff. Add the vanilla. Fold the mixture into the frozen peaches and freeze for 4 hours. Stir well after 1 hour.

Makes 1 quart.

Desserts

$\mathcal{S}$ trawberry Ice Cream

1 quart ripened strawberries, washed and hulled	**1 teaspoon unflavored gelatin**
1 cup sugar	**1 tablespoon cold water**
1 tablespoon fresh lemon juice	**1 cup milk**
¼ teaspoon salt	**3 cups light cream**

■ Puree the strawberries in a food processor to make 1¾ cups. Add the sugar, lemon juice, and salt. Blend. Cover and refrigerate.

Soften the gelatin in cold water. Stir to dissolve. In a saucepan scald the milk. Add the gelatin and let the mixture cool. Blend in the strawberry purée and cream. Pour the mixture into a freezer can. Freeze according to the manufacturer's directions.

Makes 10 servings.

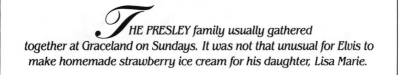

$\mathcal{T}$HE PRESLEY family usually gathered together at Graceland on Sundays. It was not that unusual for Elvis to make homemade strawberry ice cream for his daughter, Lisa Marie.

$\mathcal{S}$ trawberry Preserves

3 pints strawberries	**3 tablespoons fresh lemon juice**
2½ plus ⅓ cups sugar	

■ Wash and hull the strawberries. Place them in a saucepan. Sift ⅓ cup of sugar over the top. Add the lemon juice. Let the berries stand overnight. Add 2½ cups of sugar and heat to boiling. Cook for 7 minutes. Shake occasionally during cooking. Pour into 2 sterilized pint jars and seal.

Makes 2 pints.

 EVERAGES

Lemon Syrup for Lemonade

1½ cups sugar
4 cups water

1½ cups fresh lemon juice

■ In a saucepan combine the sugar and water and boil for 5 minutes. Cool. Add the lemon juice. Remove the seeds. Mix thoroughly and pour into a glass jar. Cover and store in the refrigerator.

To prepare lemonade with this syrup, use about ½ cup of syrup for each 8 ounce glass. Fill with crushed ice and water.

Makes 5 cups of syrup.

Lemonade

4 lemons
½ cup fresh lemon juice
½ cup sugar

16 large ice cubes, crushed
Mint to taste

■ Cut the lemons in half and remove 4 thin slices. Squeeze the remaining lemons. Remove the seeds from the juice but do not strain. Add the sugar and crushed ice. Stir until the sugar dissolves and the ice is almost melted. Garnish with lemon slices and mint. Serve immediately.

Makes 4 servings.

☆ **IN A QUIET moment at the piano**

*T*HERE had to be a reason why a generation
of kids loved Elvis Presley so much. Could it have been because Elvis led
them to believe that their future was not so bleak? Was it because he
spoke to them with a voice they could understand? Or was it because
they were looking for something and found it through his music? He
sang to them of hope, happiness, and love. He came to them at a time
when they needed someone to represent their thoughts and feelings. His
style of music stimulated them. Sure, they were nervous and screamed
when he approached them. But in the end, there stood Elvis Presley,
and he was the one they believed in.

Fit For a King

$\mathscr{L}$ imeade

10 limes
¾ cup sugar

2 cups ice water
½ teaspoon grated lime rind

■ Squeeze 9 of the limes. Remove the seeds. Do not strain the juice. Thinly slice the remaining lime. Combine the lime juice, sugar, water, and rind. Mix well. Fill a glass ⅓ full with crushed ice. Add the limeade. Garnish with slices of lime.

Makes 5 servings.

$\mathscr{G}$ rape Lemonade

½ cup fresh lemon juice
¾ cup fresh orange juice
¼ cup sugar
1¼ cups grape juice, chilled

1¾ cups ice water
Lemon slices
Mint

■ Remove the seeds from the lemon and orange juices, but do not strain. Blend in the sugar until thoroughly dissolved. Add the chilled grape juice and ice water. Place 2 tablespoons of crushed ice cubes into 5 8-ounce glasses. Fill with lemonade. Garnish with a lemon slice. Add a sprig of mint.

Makes 5 servings.

$\mathscr{H}$ ot Chocolate

2 1-ounce squares unsweetened chocolate
1⅓ cups boiling water
⅓ cup sugar

Salt to taste
2 cups evaporated milk
2 cups boiling water
½ teaspoon vanilla extract

■ In the top of a double boiler over simmering water melt the chocolate. Add 1⅓ cups of boiling water to obtain a smooth paste. Add the sugar, salt, and evaporated milk. Heat for about 5 minutes, stirring often. Add the vanilla. Whip with an electric mixer for 1 minute. Add the remaining boiling water. Serve hot. Top with whipping cream or marshmallows.

Makes 6 servings.

 ot Caramel Milk Shake

1 egg yolk
1 tablespoon caramel syrup
Salt to taste

1 cup hot milk
¼ teaspoon vanilla extract

■ In the top of a double boiler beat the egg yolk until thick. Add the syrup, salt, and milk. Place the pan over simmering water, and heat until scalding. Remove the pan from the heat. Add the vanilla and beat until frothy. Serve immediately.
    Makes 1 serving.

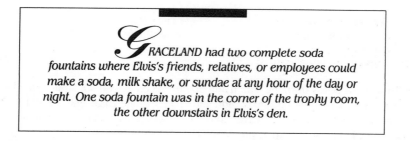

RACELAND had two complete soda fountains where Elvis's friends, relatives, or employees could make a soda, milk shake, or sundae at any hour of the day or night. One soda fountain was in the corner of the trophy room, the other downstairs in Elvis's den.

ider Cooler

1 cup apple cider, chilled
1 teaspoon sugar

Dash salt
1 scoop vanilla ice cream

■ In a mixing bowl combine the apple cider, sugar, and salt. Blend in the ice cream. Beat until the ice cream is half melted.
    Makes 1 serving.

Cranberry Cooler

1 cup ice water
¼ cup thick sweetened cranberry
   jelly
Dash salt

1 teaspoon sugar
1 teaspoon fresh lemon juice
1 large scoop vanilla ice cream

■ In a mixing bowl combine all of the ingredients except the ice cream. Blend thoroughly. Add the ice cream and blend until it is half melted.

   Makes 1 serving.

☆ AT A PRESS conference in Las Vegas in 1969

 # ruit Juice Medley

1½ cups fresh orange juice
⅓ cup fresh lemon juice
1 cup pineapple juice, chilled

2 cups ice water
Sugar to taste

■ Combine all of the ingredients and refrigerate until chilled.
Makes 6 servings.

 # ranberry Punch

1 quart fresh cranberries
4 cups water
1 cup sugar
5 whole cloves
½ teaspoon grated lemon rind

½ teaspoon grated orange rind
2 tablespoons fresh lemon juice
1 quart apple juice, chilled
1 medium orange, sliced

■ Wash the cranberries. In a saucepan bring the water to a boil. Add the cranberries, cover, and boil until the skins pop. Push the berries through a sieve. In a large mixing bowl combine the strained berries, sugar, cloves, orange rind, and lemon rind. Cover and refrigerate. Add the lemon juice and apple juice, and stir to blend. Remove the cloves before serving. Garnish with orange slices.
Makes 2½ quarts.

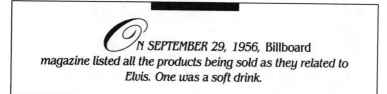

ON SEPTEMBER 29, 1956, Billboard magazine listed all the products being sold as they related to Elvis. One was a soft drink.

ot Apple Cider

1 quart sweet apple cider	**1 4-inch cinnamon stick**
8 whole allspice	**Dash salt**
8 whole cloves	**¼ cup packed light brown sugar**

■ In a saucepan combine the cider, allspice, cloves, cinnamon stick, salt, and sugar. Cover and bring the cider very slowly to boiling. The heat should be so low that it will take about 30 minutes for the cider to boil. Remove the cider from the heat and serve steaming hot. Remove the allspice, cloves, and cinnamon stick.

Makes 5 servings.

hocolate Malted Shake

½ cup chocolate syrup, chilled	**1 large scoop vanilla or chocolate**
¼ cup malted milk powder	**ice cream**
2 cups milk, chilled	**Salt to taste**

■ In a blender combine the chocolate syrup, malted milk powder, chilled milk, ice cream, and salt. Beat thoroughly until frothy. Pour into serving glasses.

Makes 2 servings.

hocolate Soda

2 tablespoons chocolate syrup	**1 large scoop vanilla or chocolate**
1 teaspoon milk	**ice cream**
½ cup carbonated water	

■ Place the chocolate syrup in a 10-ounce glass. Add the milk and ¼ cup of the carbonated water. Stir. Add the ice cream and the remaining carbonated water.

Makes 1 serving.

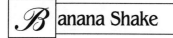

Banana Shake

1 cup milk, chilled
1 ripened banana, peeled and
   mashed
⅓ cup fresh orange juice

1 teaspoon sugar
1 large scoop vanilla ice cream
Salt to taste

■ In a blender combine the milk and mashed banana. Blend in the orange juice, sugar, ice cream, and salt. Beat throughly. Pour into serving glasses.
   Makes 1 serving.

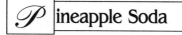

Pineapple Soda

2 tablespoons crushed pineapple
1 tablespoon sugar
Salt to taste

1 teaspoon milk
½ cup carbonated water
1 scoop vanilla ice cream

■ In a 10-ounce glass combine the pineapple juice, sugar, salt, and milk. Blend thoroughly. Add ¼ cup of carbonated water and the ice cream. Stir a few times to blend. Add the remaining carbonated water.
   Makes 1 serving.

WHEN Movie Teen Illustrated revealed "What's Eating in Elvisville?" it listed lemon meringue pie, cherry angel food cake, pork chops, hamburgers, spaghetti, and milk chocolate peanut butter cups as his favorite foods. It inventoried the beverages in his refrigerator: Pepsi, pineapple juice, Hawaiian Punch, and sasparilla.

ineapple Cooler

1 cup pineapple juice, chilled　　**Dash salt**
1 tablespoon fresh lemon juice　　**2 large scoops vanilla ice cream**

■ In a mixing bowl combine all of the ingredients except the ice cream. Blend thoroughly. Add the ice cream and blend until the ice cream is half melted. Pour into serving glasses.

Makes 2 servings.

☆ **ELVIS, who neither smoked nor drank, enjoyed a Coke.**

$\mathscr{L}$ emon Cooler

1 cup ice water
¼ cup fresh lemon juice
¼ cup sugar

Dash salt
1 large scoop vanilla ice cream

■ In a mixing bowl combine all of the ingredients except the ice cream. Blend thoroughly. Add the ice cream and blend until it is half melted. Pour into a serving glass. Makes 1 serving.

$\mathscr{B}$ lack Raspberry Shake

2 cups milk, chilled
2½ teaspoons seedless black
  raspberry jam

1 tablespoon fresh lemon juice
Salt to taste
3 small scoops vanilla ice cream

■ In a blender combine the milk, raspberry jam, lemon juice, salt, and ice cream. Beat thoroughly. Pour into serving glasses. Makes 2 servings.

$\mathscr{P}$ each Shake

½ cup canned peaches, chilled
⅓ cup milk
Salt to taste

2 drops almond extract
1 large scoop vanilla ice cream

■ Push the peaches through a sieve with their syrup. In a blender combine the peaches, milk, salt, almond extract, and ice cream. Beat until smooth. Pour into a serving glass. Makes 1 serving.

 lack Cow

4 cups rootbeer
4 teaspoons milk

4 large scoops vanilla ice cream

■ Combine ¼ cup of rootbeer and 1 teaspoon of milk in each of 4 10-ounce glasses. Add the ice cream and stir slightly. Divide the remaining rootbeer among the glasses.
   Makes 4 servings.

range Soda

¼ cup fresh orange juice
Grated orange rind
1 teaspoon fresh lemon juice
1 tablespoon sugar

1 teaspoon milk
½ cup lime soda water
1 large scoop vanilla ice cream

■ In a 10-ounce glass combine the orange juice, orange rind, lemon juice, sugar, and milk. Add ¼ cup of lime soda water and the ice cream. Mix slightly. Add the remaining lime soda water and serve immediately.
   Makes 1 serving.

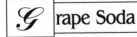 rape Soda

½ cup grape juice, chilled
2 tablespoons sugar
1 teaspoon milk

½ cup ginger ale, chilled
1 scoop vanilla ice cream

■ In a 10-ounce glass combine the grape juice, sugar, and milk. Blend thoroughly. Add ¼ cup of ginger ale and the ice cream. Stir a few times to blend. Add the remaining ginger ale.
   Makes 1 serving.

☆ TAKING a coffee break on the set of *Loving You*

Fit For a King

228

 **Eggnog**

2 eggs
¼ cup sugar
Salt to taste
2 cups milk

1 tablespoon rum extract
½ cup cream
Fresh ground nutmeg

■ In the top of a double boiler beat the eggs, sugar and salt. Add the milk. Place the pan over hot water, and stir frequently until heated through. Chill. Stir in the rum extract. Fold in the stiffly beaten cream and add a dash of nutmeg. Serve immediately.
   Makes 6 servings.

ELVIS'S friends and family knew that he drank a lot of milk, water, and soda pop. On certain occasions, he preferred chocolate milk.

 Eggnog

4 egg yolks
¼ cup sugar
3 cups milk, chilled
1 cup thin cream, chilled

1½ teaspoons vanilla
¼ teaspoon salt
Fresh ground nutmeg

■ In a mixing bowl beat the egg yolks until very thick and light. Add the sugar and beat thoroughly. Blend in the milk, cream, vanilla, and salt. Pour into 5 serving glasses. Garnish with nutmeg and serve immediately.
   Makes 5 servings.

Beverages

☆ **ELVIS in *Blue Hawaii***

"*IT'S LIKE someone just came up and told me there aren't going to be any more cheeseburgers in the world.*"
—Felton Javis, Elvis's producer, commenting on Elvis's death

GLOSSARY OF COOKING TERMS

Bake: To cook covered or uncovered in an oven.

Baste: To moisten foods during cooking with pan drippings or special sauce to add flavor and to prevent drying.

Beat: To make a mixture smooth by adding air by a brisk whipping or stirring motion using a spoon or electric mixer.

Blend: To thoroughly mix two or more ingredients until smooth and uniform.

Boil: To cook in a liquid at boiling temperature where bubbles rise to the surface and break. For a full rolling boil, bubbles form rapidly throughout the mixture.

Braise: To cook slowly with a small amount of liquid in a tightly covered pan on top of a stove or in an oven.

Broil: To cook by direct heat, usually in a broiler or over coals.

Chill: To place in a refrigerator to reduce the temperature.

Chop: To cut into pieces the size of peas with a knife, chopper, or blender.

Cool: To remove from heat and let stand at room temperature.

Cream: To beat with a spoon or electric mixer until the mixture is soft and smooth. When applied to blending shortening and sugar, the mixture is beaten until light and fluffy.

Cut In: To mix shortening with dry ingredients using a pastry blender or knives.

Dice: To cut food into small cubes or in uniform size and shape.

Dissolve: To blend a dry substance in a liquid to form a solution.

Glaze: A mixture applied to food which hardens or becomes firm and adds flavor and a glossy appearance.

Grate: To rub a grater that separates the food into very fine particles.

Julienne: To cut into long thin strips.

Marinate: To allow food to stand in a liquid to tenderize and to enhance flavor.

Mince: To cut or finely chop food into very small pieces.

Parboil: To cook partially by boiling for a brief period.

Poach: To cook in hot liquid, being careful that the food holds its shape during the cooking process.

Precook: To cook food partially or completely before final cooking or reheating.

Roast: To cook uncovered with water added, usually in an oven.

Sauté: To brown or cook in a small amount of butter or oil.

Scald: To burn in a hot liquid or steam.

Scallop: To bake foods usually in a casserole dish with sauce or other liquid.

Sear: To char, scorch, or burn the surface.

Steam: To cook in steam with or without pressure. A small amount of water is used.

Stir: To mix ingredients with a circular motion until well blended.

Toss: To mix ingredients lightly.

Whip: To beat rapidly to incorporate air and produce expansion.

$\mathcal{I}$NDEX

Fit For a King

234

Fit For a King

Fit For a King

Index